Nikola Tamindzic

ABOUT THE EDITOR

Aaron Hicklin joined *BlackBook*
as editor-in-chief after five
years with *Gear* magazine. The
author of *Boy Soldiers*, he lives
in Brooklyn, New York.

THE

REVOLUTION

WILL

BE

ACCESSORIZED

THE
REVOLUTION
WILL
BE
ACCESSORIZED

BlackBook Presents

Dispatches from the New Counterculture

Edited by Aaron Hicklin

HARPER PERENNIAL

NEW YORK • LONDON • TORONTO • SYDNEY

HARPER PERENNIAL

THE REVOLUTION WILL BE ACCESSORIZED. Copyright © 2006 by Aaron Hicklin.
All rights reserved. Printed in the United States of America. No part of this
book may be used or reproduced in any manner whatsoever without written permission except in the case of brief quotations embodied in critical
articles and reviews. For information address HarperCollins Publishers, 10
East 53rd Street, New York, NY 10022.

HarperCollins books may be purchased for educational, business, or sales
promotional use. For information please write: Special Markets Department,
HarperCollins Publishers, 10 East 53rd Street, New York, NY 10022.

FIRST EDITION

Designed by Justin Dodd

Library of Congress Cataloging-in-Publication Data is available upon request.

ISBN-10: 0-06-084732-8
ISBN-13: 978-0-06-084732-6

06 07 08 09 10 ❖/RRD 10 9 8 7 6 5 4 3 2 1

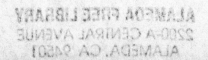

CONTENTS

PREFACE

Karl "King" Wenclas, irascible leader of the Underground Literary Alliance, will be pained by *BlackBook*'s first anthology. Not only have we chosen to include Bruno Maddox's cheerful skewering of the Alliance—which came to notoriety by ambushing New York's literary elite in a series of headline-grabbing stunts—but the contents reads like a ULA hit list. Wenclas, who favors soap opera realism over irony and wit, would not enjoy Sam Lipsyte's indulgent riff on April Fool's Day, or Ryan Boudinot's dark comedy, "My Mother Was a Monster," which is neither remotely realistic nor instructive. He would positively despise the fact that his bête noire, Rick Moody, is among those who answered the call of our "Hemingway Challenge," especially as it manages to reference such bourgeois concerns as France and cheese in its scant six words. And he would find the tendency to dwell on fashion despicably frivolous. He would, perhaps, have a point, but *BlackBook* is a singular hybrid, a style magazine with a literary soul. Naomi Klein, in her exchange with Douglas Coupland, pays us a backhanded compliment by describing *BlackBook* as a "mutant breed." We chose not to be offended. Mutants are okay, the product of competing but, ultimately, complimentary desires. In our case it is a faintly quixotic marriage of literary aspiration with a downtown fashion aesthetic. Where Klein sees "downtown" as a cynical marketing ploy, we see it as a way of looking at the world, a spirited enthusiasm for urban life, and the ways in which fashion, pop culture, and politics intersect and sometimes collide. If that has sometimes served to muddy the waters, well, we like it that way. While the magazine pool has become ever more segmented—all the better to send clear signals to advertisers—*BlackBook* still enjoys frolicking in the shallows as well as in the deep end. We may be "dripping in ink" (Naomi Klein again), but gloss and substance are not mutually exclusive. Like Joan Didion's conversation with Meghan Daum, which covers the gamut from the Iraq war to buying a winter coat on Condé Nast wages, we like to mix it up. That conversation, incidentally, is included here in part because it touches on the nature of writing itself. Invited to explain why Didion writes, she gets straight to the point: To figure out what I'm thinking.

Figuring out what we're thinking is a pretty good description of the editorial process at *BlackBook*, where each issue is designed to focus around a particular theme. For that reason, perhaps, some of the best entries have a relaxed and transient quality you would expect from a good conversation, drawing frequently from personal experience to illuminate a broader point. Indeed, as with Didion and Daum, several of the pieces are actual conversations, including one in which artists Jeff Koons and Matthew Barney discuss the complicated relationship between art and their own celebrity, and another in which Brit Art meets Brit Lit, in the form of Damien Hirst and Irvine

Welsh exchanging notes on working methods, reality TV, and drug use. Although these pieces are connected primarily by the fact of being published in *BlackBook*, the title of this anthology references a recurring theme: the relationship between fashion and politics, and personal identity and the wider world. It is exemplified in the conversation between Klein and Coupland but it also manifests in contributions from Daum, Glenn O'Brien, and Dirk Wittenborn, among others. Even the pieces that don't address it explicitly reflect a preoccupation with the tension between authenticity and artifice, integrity and compromise. In one particular case—JT LeRoy's account of traveling to the Congo with William T. Vollmann—issues of artifice and integrity would now seem even more pronounced than they were at the time of publication, when we added an editor's note suggesting that the entire piece was fabricated. We chose to include it because it was written with a flair that is authentic even if the author is not. In any case, we would never claim that all of these stories are important; some, in fact, are downright silly—*BlackBook* is a pop culture magazine, after all—but they are, we hope, never less than stimulating, provocative, and, best of all, entertaining.

This anthology owes itself in large part to the collective efforts of an exceptional editorial team, including Jordan Heller and Meg Thomann, but it also reflects the impressive contributions of successive editors who laid the groundwork for the magazine that *BlackBook* is today. It would not have been possible without Anuj Desai, Bill Powers, and Evan Schindler. A special thanks as well to the rest of the current team, including Stephanie Waxlax, photography director; Eddie Brannan, art director; Elizabeth Sulcer, fashion director; and Jess Holl, managing editor; who have made working at *BlackBook* such an enjoyable and collaborative exercise. That exercise, of course, would be redundant without the writers who contribute such a wealth of great stories for rather less than minimum wage. You are brilliant, and we never forget it. Finally, because independent magazines are such a privileged breed, many thanks to Eric Gertler, Ari Horrowitz, and Jyl Elias, who pay our salaries and let us get on with it.

—AARON HICKLIN

INTRODUCTION

Ten years is a long life span for a magazine, particularly a little magazine—one aimed at a niche community. When I saw the first issue of *BlackBook* in 1996, with its black cover, I remember thinking that it wouldn't survive the year, let alone the millennium, although I was grateful for the fact that there was no movie star on the cover. (*BlackBook* has since had actors and even movie stars on the cover, but they're mostly the right sort of movie star—*our* kind of movie star: Benicio Del Toro, Scarlett Johansson, and Naomi Watts.) And somehow it's going strong ten years later. Scofield Thayer's *Dial*—which published Djuna Barnes, E. E. Cummings, Bertrand Russell, Kenneth Burke, Gaston Lachaise, and W. B. Yeats, in its first year of publication, in 1921—expired in 1929. Ford Maddox Ford's *Transatlantic Review* (Hemingway, Joyce, and Pound) lasted just a year and a half. And the *Soho Weekly News*, the stridently unglossy precursor to *BlackBook* (Patti Smith on Television, Lester Bangs on *London Calling*), which presided over the birth of the downtown aesthetic, and the very concept of "downtown," published from October 1973 to March 1982. That same year *Details* hoved into view. I speak of course of the pre–Condé Nast publication that Annie Flanders founded to cover downtown nightlife in the Mudd Club era.

Magazines like the *Soho Weekly News*, *Details*, and *Paper* arose out of a specific time and place—downtown Manhattan—and helped to define the community that they were covering. (Ditto the *Face*, the hip British "style" bible, which ushered in the 1980s and helped forge a synthesis of counterculture and consumer culture that seemed radical at the time and now seems like the status quo.) They were the house organs of an intersecting set of salons that held their provisional headquarters in nightclubs like Area, galleries like Mary Boone's, and restaurants like Odeon. They chronicled the rise of a new bohemia that was operating beneath the radar of the mainstream press (which in retrospect was clearly a blessing). *Time* magazine couldn't help noticing Studio 54, which was in its own backyard, a few blocks from the magazine's offices, but they sure as hell weren't writing about the Pyramid or Save the Robots. *BlackBook* is in obvious ways the successor to all of these publications, although at this point "downtown" has almost ceased to be a physical location—Manhattan south of Fourteenth Street—and has become (uh-oh) a sensibility.

Downtown is now Williamsburg and South Beach and Silver Lake and pretty much anywhere else. A cynical reader back in 1996 might well have asked whether that sensibility hadn't already been thoroughly reified and co-opted by the uptown merchants and media. The answer, of course, is yes and no. And the fact is that if *BlackBook* resembles *Vanity Fair*, *Vogue*, or *Rolling Stone* in its production values, it doesn't look like, or read like, any of them. The magazine is almost too glossy and too beautiful for its own good, and for its own progressive and transgressive ambitions—somebody should either shoot the art director or give him a raise. But it's the kind of magazine that's alive to its own contradictions and seems to devote some of its pages to exploring them (see the exchange between Douglas Coupland and Naomi Klein, discussing among other things the authenticity of *BlackBook* and trying to fix its coordinates at the intersection of fashion and advertising).

The mix of downtown fashion sensibility and literary ambition can seem a little lumpy. The fall 2003 "Protest" issue attempts to mix fashion and radical politics—with models posing as protestors and Scarlett Johansson looking almost Maoist on the cover. But some of the best pieces published in the magazine are in one way or another exploring and teasing out these kinds of contradictions. Like Glenn O'Brien's "If It Makes You Think, Is It Fashion?" To quote, "An organized form of narcissism, fashion distracts the population from economics, ecology, and 'current events.' Who needs to worry about the Sudan when we've got John Galliano?" And Megan Daum, in Los Angeles, finds a geographical analogue for the whole question of authenticity and its discontents, "Moving to Los Angeles is a bit like becoming a Republican. It is also, especially for New Yorkers, the ultimate bourgeois act."

What makes the magazine more than a downtown "style" bible and guide to nightlife, which has lost much of its originality, is the writing. I'm not sure where else I could read Dirk Wittenborn's "When Ass Kissing Became Networking." Or Toby Young's "Demon Club Soda." Or Emma Forrest's "*Harold and Maude* Is Forever." But pieces like these—which are smart and funny and self-conscious all at once—would seem to justify the entire enterprise, even without the nightclub listings and the titillating glimpses of what most won't be wearing to Marquee and Bungalow 8 next season. If avatars of the avant-garde tend to be humorless, *BlackBook* tends to go toward the other extreme and thereby, possibly, saves itself from terminal hipness.

—JAY McINERNEY

THE **REVOLUTION** WILL BE **ACCESSORIZED**

L.A. Bourgeois

MEGHAN DAUM

One recent morning I was sitting at my desk in my home in Los Angeles when the telephone rang. The display on the caller ID said Sandra Bernhard and indicated a number in the Greater L.A. Metro. I took in a minor gasp. The actress/comedienne Sandra Bernhard, who has always occupied a place on my altar of celebrity worship, was calling me. What could she want? Perhaps she had read something of mine, a book or an article, and wanted to work with me on a project. Maybe she was developing a cable television show or radio program or humor book about some cultural malady she thought I'd relate to, like chronic misanthropy or dry skin or dogs that shed. Perhaps she knew someone I knew—how many degrees of separation could there be between Sandra Bernhard and me?—and wanted to "touch base," "put a call in," issue forth some recognition of our shared sensibilities, invite me out for coffee to talk about the possibility of collaboration, or whatever, you know, just say hi. It was a Monday morning, the first day back to work after a long holiday weekend, and as the ringing phone vibrated in my palm the promise of good fortune buzzed through me like caffeine.

The days had been unremarkable of late. A slow September had folded into a slower October and November, the lack of seasons erasing any sense of urgency or passage of time. But there I was, on the first day of December, receiving a call from Sandra Bernhard, who was possibly calling because she wanted to option an obscure article I'd written for an obscure magazine, who possibly suspected I was a person whom she should get to know, who possibly wanted to be my friend, possibly very soon. There was a rightness about it all, a karmic logic, proof, finally, that things really did turn around when one was patient. This entire sequence of thoughts passed through my mind in the time it took for the phone to ring two times. I waited through the third ring to answer, preparing an air of vocal insouciance that would conceal my euphoric anticipation.

It was Blanca Castillo, my cleaning lady. She was calling to ask if she could come on Saturday rather than Friday. In my shock, I barely listened to her. I wondered if Sandra Bernhard was right there, puttering around in leather pants and Manolos while Blanca stole away to the telephone. I wondered if Sandra Bernhard was neater than I was, if Blanca preferred her to me, if Blanca worked for celebrities throughout the week and saw me as a kind of charity case, a neophyte in the realm of domestic employment. Though she's been in this country for almost twenty years, Blanca's English is halting and uncertain, and as she stumbled through an apologetic explanation of why she couldn't come on Friday I felt a chemical shift inside myself; the euphoria vanished as quickly as it had appeared. The disappointment was almost overwhelming. Sandra Bernhard had not called me. It was another Monday, another month. Soon it would be another year. Still the sun shined.

I cannot take this anecdote any further without explaining that before moving to Los Angeles, nearly a year ago, I'd never employed outside help to clean my house. I grew up in a family whose liberal guilt collided with its midwestern origins with such thunderous intensity that I was thirty before I ever drove (unsure of what to do) into a car wash and thirty-three before I considered the possibility that paying someone twenty dollars an hour to perform services for which they actively advertise and/or take referrals is not necessarily on a par with running a sweatshop. Still, I can't help feeling that employing a cleaner represents some kind of foray into a phase of my life that might look something like adulthood but has more to do with the simulation of movie and magazine spread life that is at the root of the current American bourgeois construct. In recent years, I have come to own or lease a number of entities that would have been unthinkable during the prebourgeois years of my twenties. I have a house, a car, an eighty-pound collie–St. Bernard mix, and a sofa that I purchased at Crate and Barrel. And since I have reluctantly decided that the dog sheds more hair in the house than I can keep under control while fulfilling my own professional responsibilities, I enlist Blanca twice a month to perform duties that, prior to the Reagan era, the vast majority of Americans managed to do on their own quite nicely. This isn't anything I'm proud of; the fact that I cannot keep my own house clean strikes me as more than a minor character flaw. But if I've discovered anything since moving to Los Angeles it's that the assimilation process feels a lot like the aging process: We mellow out, we settle down, we accept, as a yoga teacher might say, "our possibilities and our limitations." Put another way, I could say we lose our edge, become resigned, learn not to flinch so visibly at the price of real estate. Which is to say, for better or worse, we let the tides of bourgeois culture crash over our rough spots until we're smooth as stones. Then we hire someone to clean up all the debris on the beach.

It feels not entirely accidental that my foray into the bourgeoisie coincides with my arrival in Los Angeles. This is a city that is bourgeois by necessity, less for its codependent relationship with the automobile than with its desperate love affair with the home. When you inhabit a geography that is at once so sprawling and so congested, when the prospect of going to a concert or a ball game or a dinner party often means an hour or more on crowded, menacing freeways, the home becomes the primary focus of leisure activity. If there's anything Angelenos enjoy more than going out, it's staying in. And as much as the rest of the world might perceive Los Angeles as a city obsessed with cars, locals know that the car is simply a means to our most precious end: our houses. The amount of time discussing paint samples and Pergo rugs and the proper, earthquake-safe bolting of water heaters makes the topic of Lexuses (or it is Lexi?) and BMWs as incidental and irrelevant as the weather. Cars, like the seventy-degree sunny days, are merely an ongoing condition. The house, be it a Brentwood estate or a slab-like bungalow in

South Central, is a living organism. And it is the house, more than the cars or clothes or Botox or anything else associated with L.A.'s celebrated materialism, that supplies the canvas for our bourgeois expression. We redecorate, we remodel, we refinance. Whether we're spending $100,000 on a new kitchen or $40 on a designer doormat, we all have the opportunity to assert some symbol of affluence. That's because the bourgeois lifestyle is no longer exclusively the domain of the bourgeoisie.

Though the term *proletariat* has become quaint, even politically incorrect, the fact that forty-three million Americans lack medical insurance is, on its own, evidence that social and economic disenfranchisement is alive and well. When Karl Marx wrote that "the modern bourgeoisie is itself the product of a long course of development, a series of revolutions in the modes of production and exchange," he could have easily been talking about the corporate monoliths that now sell us the Indian jewelry and shabby chic furniture that deliver an aura of hipness without the hassle of rummaging through flea markets. But anyone who's shopped for a blender or even cotton underwear in the last several years has been wooed by the slick, shiny packaging in which our current mode of production and exchange is wrapped. There's a lot of cool stuff out there that's not very expensive. The economic course of the twenty-first century has helped to spread, if not the wealth itself, at least the trappings of that wealth into farther reaches of the culture than Marx could have imagined.

The revolution did indeed come. It's just that it was a revolution not of politics, but of style. Any democratic presidential candidate who's scratching his head wondering why the lower and working classes continually vote against their economic interests would do well to visit a Target store. Target, as most of us now know, is less a store than a phenomenon. It is what makes the poor really invisible. It makes them look just like the rich. In fact, at Target the poor shop right alongside the rich. If ever there was a symbol of the democratization of design, of the sudden ability of the average or even poorer-than-average American to appear affluent it is the fact that a sleek, conspicuously modish Michael Graves Spinner Whistle Teakettle can be purchased at more than 1,100 Target stores across the country for $29.99. Gone are the days when the rich had lustrous kitchen appliances and the poor made do with garage sale items. Never before have so many of us been able to join this game of bourgeois dress-up. If the *Roseanne* show were still on the air today, the working-class Connor family might have a Michael Graves teakettle. At the very least, its costumers and set designers would note that an Isaac Mizrahi zipped cardigan hoodie can be picked up for $24.99 and Cynthia Rowley and Ilene Rosenzweig's Swell line offers a smartly chic fabric shower curtain for a mere $14.99.

As I write this, a giant Target is being built on an entire city block in Hollywood, just a few miles away from where I live. This is a prospect that excites not only me but dozens of friends and acquaintances who view the opening of a new, convenient Target location as a major asset to our quality of life. The frequency with which Target comes up in conversation, while amusing, is not exactly surprising. Now that the dues of bourgeoisie membership exist on a sliding scale, most of us can afford to stay in the club. This gives us all a common reference point, a safety zone in which we can discuss our consumer habits and tastes without fear of alienating others or appearing elitist. The reality that there is a yawning gap between the rich and the poor, the fact that a rich person's Target experience (a playground of items that seem practically free!) bears little resemblance to the required discipline and inherent anxiety of a poor person's Target experience can be easily dismissed. What matters is that we all have the same teakettle.

I've been known to use the word "bourgey." I use it as a derogatory expression connoting various cultural forces that I and others of my ilk deem loathsomely middlebrow. By "ilk" I mean people who spent their late teens and much of their twenties engaged in a violent struggle to keep at bay anything that's less than hip. We are people who have had the luxury of a certain kind of educational or class privilege and, as I see in retrospect, used that privilege as a means of rejecting almost everything in our midst rather than taking advantage of the myriad options that lay before us. That is to say we only liked things until the rest of the world liked them; then we hated them. Every generation keeps its own list of treasonous icons—the bands that get too popular, the authors that dare to write best sellers, the sneaker styles that suddenly show up in the mall. That I continue, on occasion, to trot out the "bourgey" allegation surely points to some form of arrested development. It also roots me firmly within my age group. The things I find middlebrow are usually things my parents' generation embraced as symbols of their cultural or socioeconomic prowess. It runs the gamut: bagel slicers, Volvos, Garrison Keillor. It's also about as moot as anything could possibly be. As anyone who's over the age of twenty-seven (thirty-four if you live in a major metropolitan area) knows, today's highbrow is tomorrow's middlebrow. The brows descend along with the rest of the sagging face; that's why it's called growing up.

Insofar as going bourgeois reflects the aging process itself, we may be forced to reconcile it as a simple fact of life. Not being twenty-one anymore means coping with the fact that the stuff you like is probably considered fogeyish by those who are twenty-one. In my less self-conscious moments, I can even admit to myself that I kind of like Volvos and Garrison Keillor, that given the choice between Garrison Keillor and, say, 90 percent of what's on the radio at any given time, I'd buy a ticket to Lake Wobegon and stay there until spring. To grow older is to accept that bourgeois is in the eye of the beholder, that "bourginess" is less an objective description than a way of calibrating our relationship to culture at large. But I think what dogs us, at least what occasionally gnaws at me when I'm sitting in my car (Subaru) listening to music that might pass for easy listening and fretting about how I still haven't read *The Tin Drum* is the anxiety stirred by the fear of becoming one of them. Even as the universe expands, the world shrinks. The more connected we become, the more we know about stuff. And the more stuff is known about the more bourgeois it becomes.

Not being twenty-one anymore means I'd be lying if I said that was all bad. Some of it, like the anxiety about my music in the car, is a waste of energy. Other parts of it may just be residual flotsam from the consumer carnival of the 1980s. In other words, it's Ronald Reagan who made me one of them. The degree to which the economic policies of the Reagan administration lay the groundwork for the democracy of tea kettle design occurred to me last December during a broadcast of the TV movie *The Reagans*. Amid an otherwise unremarkable sequence of biographical snippets about the couple's rise from Hollywood B-listers to the White House came a scene wherein Ron and Nancy, up late after attending a Republican fund-raiser, mull over the ramifications of leaving the Democratic Party.

> **RON:** I like those people tonight. You know? They were really nice. Don't you think?
>
> **NANCY:** And rich.
>
> **RON:** I've never seen so many rich people in one place.
>
> **NANCY:** Yeah, it was a whole new level. Real money.
>
> **RON:** Yeah, different. Texaco. Shell. Mobile oil. And they didn't even look tired. You know? They look like they spend all their time on vacation. Nice fellas.

This exchange still leaves me with an uncanny déjà vu. I've heard this conversation somewhere before (minus the references to big oil and Senate campaigns). I've heard almost these exact words in more conversations than I can count and it's never exactly about switching political affiliations; it's been about moving to Los Angeles. Most often, it is how New Yorkers sound when they contemplate moving to Los Angeles. The thought sequence is nearly always the same, as formulaic and intoxicating as a pop song. There is the initial suspicion of the apparent ease of it all (it can't be as good as it looks) and then there is the initial seduction of the weather (warm but generally not too warm, dry and sunny and moodless—weather on Prozac). Then the Californians begin their seduction. They're really nice, don't you think? They're rich. Even the ones who aren't rich seem rich. Such lovely homes, such lawn maintenance, such friendly dogs that don't leave a trace of hair on the sofa. They don't even look tired. You know?

Moving to Los Angeles is a bit like becoming a Republican. It is also, especially for New Yorkers, the ultimate bourgeois act. There is an element to living here that involves a certain hanging up of bohemian credentials, a surrender to the strip malls and car culture and suburb-oriented infrastructure that rankles those of us who purport to be "against" such things. As unimaginative a political position as this is, it can't be denied that L.A., for all its corners of funky, urban grit (see: the tattooed hipsters of Silver Lake and Echo Park), will probably never shake its reputation for bottle blond wannabe starlets and drug-addled, mansion dwelling lotharios. Despite a formidable, albeit subtle intellectual community in Los Angeles, the city's brand recognition remains tied around a celebrated American stereotype: the general flakiness of Californians and the more particular (and insidious) shallowness of Angelenos.

Since I'm not one to deny most stereotypes their God-given kernels of truth, I will admit to running up against slightly more air-headedness in Los Angeles than I have in other parts of the country. Maybe it's the automobile-induced isolation, maybe it's the lulling effects of weatherlessness, but certain Angelenos, for some reason, like to talk about astrology and spirit guides and gurus and scientology. This is their brand of bohemianism. And the speed with which this bohemianism has been converted to the bourgeois (see: the yoga aisle at Target) has less to do with shallowness than with a kind of willingness to grow up. Angelenos, as a group, do not rail against the bourgeois affectations of Garrison Keillor; they sit back in their cars and drink him in. They do not shout at each other in a crowded supermarket; they take a breath, find their balance, and say a prayer of thanks for all of life's blessings—for instance the availability of a certain perfectly good table wine that sells in California for $1.99. As a New Yorker at heart, and a snob to the core, I can feel my edges being sanded down by these blessings and I don't always like it. But I try to chalk up this dichotomy to yin and yang of the East Coast–West Coast continuum. What are the coasts if not the most tangible manifestations of the opposite sides of the cultural spectrum? What is California if not the epitome of the West, of the other edge, of leftness itself? What is Los Angeles if not the corporate headquarters of that edge, the McWest, a mammoth left turn lane on Bourgey Boulevard?

What California is and, more important, what Los Angeles represents to the vast majority of its residents, is an exhilarating merger of middle-class values and upper-class aesthetics. If Target were a city of eight million it would be Los Angeles, a place where ambition is expressed through appearance and form trumps function any day of the week. The rather cumbersome ergonomics of the Michael Graves teakettle present the same contradiction as the million-dollar house perched ludicrously on the Malibu mudslide; it may not last forever, but it sure looks nice. At the same time, there are plenty of ordinary things to choose from here. For every Porsche there are a thousand Toyotas. For every nipped and tucked Beverly Hills maven, there are a thousand office girls just trying to pay the rent in Torrance. The beauty in all of this lies in the degree to which everyone can absorb the glamour. With bourgeois sprinkled so evenly throughout the atmosphere, descending upon every man, woman, and child like ashes from the wild fires, the democracy of design can give us the illusion of real democracy.

Los Angeles's chief export may be the movies, but its local economy is largely in the business of lifestyle. The gleaming cars—never rusty or mud splattered—the generically attractive citizenry, the conspicuous yet largely unmentioned racial seg-regation all conspire to make the city look like a soundstage in the very movies that sell that lifestyle to the rest of the world. The degree to which my house looks like a movie set (albeit, given my minimalist tendencies, the set of *Witness*) has less to do with any particular decorating skills than with the value—some might say the moral value—I have come to place on the beauty of things. Like so many others here, I have come to answer the question "why do you like L.A.?" by listing any num-ber of visual effects: the pink sunsets over the palm trees, the twinkles of mid-century moderns in the nighttime hills, the way every stoplight offers a slide show of passing drivers. It's a voyeur's paradise, a thousand stories unfolding behind glass: Here is a man on his cell phone, here is a couple laughing, here is a mother with her child. These streams of traffic are our versions of snowflakes, dissipating into the background, replaced in an instant, no two ever alike.

I answer the question "why do you like L.A.?" the same way I'd answer the question "why do you like the United States?" I like it because for all its hypocrisy, for all its unnaturalness, for all the lies it sends to the rest of the world, it has found a way to wrap itself around the human ego like the sweetest sleeping partner. It nuzzles us when we need it to. It rolls over and gives us room when we need our space. Its flatters us with its company, separating us from some fantasy of ourselves by only the tiniest increments. My phone rings and, for a moment, Sandra Bernhard is my new best friend. The next second, the tables have turned. Blanca Castillo needs to reschedule. Blanca Castillo is in the home of a celebrity. Blanca Castillo, though she lives in a cruel world where people do not clean up after themselves, is absorbing the most base form of American glamour, the glamour of celebrity, and I, in turn, am absorbing it from her.

Is this not, in the end, the road map to bourgeois life? What are we if not vessels of our aspirations? What is America if not an agrarian nation that feeds the world our fantasies along with our corn? Los Angeles feeds us in the best and worse possible ways. It lets us pretend ordinary people can look like movie stars. It turns our tea kettles into objects of beauty, our limitations into possibilities. It lets us grow up gracefully, unburdened by seasons, absolved of guilt, safe from the dark corners that house the damage we inflict. Every day the poor get poorer. And every morning the teakettle whistles and the fog burns off and the sun shines.

When Ass Kissing Became Networking

DIRK WITTENBORN

When I was a boy, getting to know a person because of what they could do for you was what my father called ass kissing. My mother called it social climbing. To me, it was brown-nosing. Now it's called networking. If it were just a matter of nomenclature, you know, like firing a bunch of people's asses and calling it "down-sizing," or using the words "extreme discomfiture" for agonizing pain, I wouldn't mind. But to me it's somehow dangerous when a pejorative suddenly becomes a positive. Now, before I start sounding like Andy Rooney, I want to make it clear I have great respect for men and women who fuck one another to get ahead. It's one of the things I like most about Los Angeles. But when you're fucking somebody to get a job, a holiday on a yacht, a ride in a private jet, it's a straightforward and pleasurable exchange for both parties involved. But to pretend to be someone's friend, to be interested in them as a person, to share their pain for personal gain is a nightmare that brings to mind the haunting verse in George Orwell's *1984*: "Under the spreading chestnut tree, I sold you and you sold me."

Networking has replaced shop in high school curriculums across the country. Parents now talk to their children about networking the way they used to sit down and tell them the facts of life. An editor at one of the most prominent literary magazines in America confessed that when her parents talked to her about what universities she should apply to, the primary consideration was not what great men or women of science and letters they might have the chance to study under, but where she would find the most profitable networking opportunities. I've been told that at one of New York City's elite private schools, fourth-graders are taught how to use BlackBerrys so they can keep track of their prepubescent platinum connections.

When did this happen to us? Is it something they put in the water along with the fluoride? Does it have something to do with the fact that the closest thing we have to a national religion is shopping? And that mega-malls have become our substitute for cathedrals? Or is it just part of the devolution of the human race? How this happened will probably always remain a mystery. But we owe it to ourselves to at least figure out when it occurred. Values don't shift like the San Andreas Fault. It wasn't an overnight change. Pods weren't suddenly placed under our beds. It was a gradual slide. As with the other great catastrophes our planet has suffered—meteors that rendered dinosaurs extinct, the Ice Age, the Black Death—history demands that we record the date when life on the planet suffers a serious setback.

I first heard the word on a hot, sweaty summer Friday in New York City in 1979. My friend, the late, great, comedienne Gilda Radner (it's important to point out here that name-dropping is a far lesser vice than networking) found herself stuck in the city, in need of transport to East Hampton. The jitneys were booked, renting a car a hassle, and never one to flaunt her celebrity, Gilda passed on a limo and resigned herself to taking the train. I remember her kvetching to me and anyone else who would listen about the difficulties involved in taking a train to the east end of Long Island—you know, figuring out the schedules, remembering to switch trains, etc., etc., etc. A young woman, new to New York, who worked for one of Gilda's friends, overheard all this, and announced that she was driving out to East Hampton and would be glad to give Gilda a lift. Four and a half hours of hideous bumper-to-bumper traffic on the Long Island Expressway gave them plenty of time for small talk. And by the time she dropped Gilda off in East Hampton, the two women were sort of friends. Or at least, that's how it seemed to Gilda until she discovered that this young woman, contrary to the impression she'd given, didn't have any plans or place to stay in East Hampton and that, in fact, immediately after saying goodbye to Gilda, had turned around and driven straight back to New York City.

I remember a puzzled Gilda treating a group of us to an hysterical rendition of the incident over dinner. She asked, "What was that about . . . what was she doing?" And I recall a voice from the other end of the table answering out of the darkness, "Networking."

I knew we were in an epidemic when Jerry Rubin, the political activist of Chicago 7 fame, began throwing official "networking" parties at Studio 54. It was about that time I began to think about the word itself. I mean, I knew there were TV networks and networks of spies . . . but networking? When you examined the social interactions, it was the perfect expression for the relationships that were being pursued. *Net*, meaning there's a profit, and *working*, indicating that a networker is never wasting time making small talk.

The economic upswing of the 1980s, the leveraged buyout boom, and the "greed is good" ethos made networkers rich. There was profit in phoniness, no doubt about it. I found myself part of a generation for whom "What Makes Sammy Run" wasn't a cautionary tale, but a primer for stooping to conquer. I remember rereading *Death of a Salesman* and thinking when Willy Loman talks about the importance of being "well liked," he may have been pathetic/tragic in the 1950s, but now he was a goddamn visionary.

There's an element of class warfare to networking. Artists, writers, and rich people have always done it, but in private, at least in the expatriate community. It was a dirty secret among the privileged. Everybody did it, but no one was proud of it. Belonging to the vast middle class Americans once took pride in, I was brought up thinking there was something sinful about social climbing. The Puritan myth that what made America great was making it on your own merit rather than who you knew was a fairy tale designed to keep the worker bees in line. It was only when the bourgeoisie began to ass lick with the efficiency and aggressiveness of their betters that it became networking.

One of the great things about being a writer is that you can't really do very much for anyone and therefore are rarely victimized by the networker. However, you are particularly vulnerable to that most toxic practitioner of this parlor bloodsport: the stealth networker—he who befriends you not for anything you can do, but for what your more successful friends can do for him. They ride you into parties like giant pigeon mites, sucking just enough blood from you to make you feel loved, then dropping you and attaching themselves to the first person you introduce them to who has a plumper, juicier, more profitable curriculum vitae.

I'll admit that I have networked and will network again. The only thing that separates me from the rest of the vermin is shame. Don't get me wrong. This doesn't mean I'm about to become a born again Christian. Rather, it just makes me a reluctant member of the bourgeoisie.

Douglas Coupland vs. Naomi Klein

T welve years ago, Douglas Coupland created an instant classic with *Generation X*, his novel of disaffected twentysomethings contemplating an empty, irony-laden future of McJobs and designer furniture. Since then his novels have reflected an unerring instinct to tap into the shifting moods and preoccupations of the time. His latest, *Hey Nostradamus!*, is no exception. Taking a high school massacre as a jumping-off point to explore Christian fundamentalism, it's a compassionate, wry treatise on spirituality from a man who once wrote that religion was like LEGO—"you have to build it yourself."

Like Coupland, Naomi Klein is concerned with ways of being in a world made sick with logos and superficial surfaces. *No Logo*, published in 2001, was the most electrifying call-to-arms since Rachel Carson's *Silent Spring* in the 1960s. Described as "a movement bible" by the *New York Times*, and "the Das Kapital of the growing anticorporate movement" by the United Kingdom's *Observer* newspaper, it helped galvanize tens of thousands of people around the world to protest big business and globalization, and turned Klein into the leading figurehead of the first true movement of the twenty-first century.

Douglas Coupland: *BlackBook* is so glossy it drips ink. It's mostly esoteric and experimental fashion ads, but fashion ads nonetheless. It's so over the top that I don't think you can say that it's like *Elle or* Vogue.

Naomi Klein: It's certainly a mutant breed. I bought the "Protest Issue" with its "Viva La Fashionista" photo shoot—models screaming silently in megaphones and holding up meaningless placards. I was so repulsed that I almost bailed from this discussion. We need radical political change, and I can't stand seeing the idea of dissent used as an accessory for Diesel.

DC: My thinking is that after a certain point, magazines like *BlackBook* are no longer in fashion territory—that they're actually appealing to a specific, small transnational style tribe that uses fashion codes as a password into its collective speakeasy.

NK: I see it as a tragic statement about American alienation: You have these editors who commission touching articles about peace, freedom, and death by Yoko Ono and Ivy Meeropol (the granddaughter of Julius and Ethel Rosenberg). But these little messages are asphyxiated by all the overproduced, over-the-top, decadent ads and fashion spreads. It makes the articles feel like Post-it notes in comparison. It's as if someone's basement zine had been cut and pasted at random into the pages of *Vogue*.

DC: Have you been on many fashion shoots? All anyone talks about is cosmetic surgery, sex, celebrity blisters, celebrity addictions, and who's traveled where the most times. Imagine Pebbles Flintstone saying the following two sentences: "If the Delta First Class Lounge in Miami runs out of ice cubes one more time, I'll give birth to fetal pigs on the spot. Oh—have you seen the Groucho Club's redecoration?" Yet at the same time it's fine, because fashion people are, to a good extent, one of the few sectors of creative culture still engaged in creating images with a power to resonate, for better or worse. I cut them slack. Fashion's okay. It's advertising I worry about. Fashion's about the soul trying to locate beauty while coping with irony and history. Advertising is essentially manipulative and exploitative.

NK: I get your point, but I fear we are past the point where the two can be separated. Either way, here we are, trying to have a dialogue and save face when we know it's going to end up sandwiched between pages dripping with ink.

DC: Hypocrisy! Well, a discussion like this for other magazines would be awkward, yet this one doesn't feel that way. "Gee—an article in *BlackBook* will sell lots of copies of books for me!" Obviously not. But it's a seductive venue where you can say whatever you want, while pretending to be a cog in the lipo-industrial complex. It's like *Interview* was in the 1970s. In *Adbusters* it would only be converting the converted; in *Elle* it would be incongruous and clunky; in *Newsweek* or something similar it would feel like a Kent Brockman editorial on the *Simpsons*. Yet there seems to be nothing sell-outy about this venue: "I can't believe Naomi Klein did a project with a fashion magazine like *BlackBook*!"—it doesn't quite work here. Why do you think this is? I think it's because fashion can provide some sense of camouflage for other ideas.

NK: Well, I'm pretty ambivalent, as you can tell. But I spend most of my time with activists, so I get accused of selling out all the time. I'm used to it and I actually enjoy the debates about where to draw the line between protecting your personal "purity" like some museum piece and getting dirty in the real/unreal world and talking to new people. In this particular case, I just think you and I are both suckers because we aren't getting paid for this "sell out," so that makes me feel both less compromised and more stupid.

DC: I did an ad for Absolut back in the 1990s. It was a ten-thousand-dollar fund-raiser, all of which went to the Western Canada Wilderness Committee, but everyone thinks I took the money and bought black market designer stem cells while laughing at poor people. God. I should have had the photo taken of me handing them one of those huge dummy checks, the letters done in that log-like font. Here was one chance where I could, and I got royally screwed over by the press.

NK: One of things I really like about your books is that you are always playing with these tensions. Your novels often end with futuristic, almost bloodless characters managing to break through the straitjackets of irony and technology to achieve a connection that's both human and sensory—in nature, or in their relationships with each other. Do you think that's the way it has to be? Are we stuck in this cycle of dressing up in spacesuits to make a simple connection?

DC: I think so. I think the only direction we can go is forward, even if it means space suits, be they designer or non-designer. In my lifetime here in Vancouver, snow has vanished, my mother is ambushed daily by e-porn, the local grocery sells nine types of mushrooms, my nephew is taught Cantonese in grade one, and pre-clearance to enter the United States at the airport now takes up to two hours, as opposed to five minutes three years ago. It's only going to get weirder. Half the trees here will be dead within two decades from imported parasites and stress. We'll soon run out of fresh water. God only knows what political nightmares lurk. I was driving along the Trans-Canada yesterday and I thought to myself, "Gee, we're finally in the future." It sounds hokey but, well, we *are*. What can I change as an individual?

What is it futile to try to change? Those two questions are the most exciting and commitment-laden.

NK: Speaking of which, we're supposed to talk about "the future of subversion," whatever that means.

DC: Oh, God. Wait—if I hear about nanobots, file encryption, or other sci-fi stuff, I'll freak. Naomi, I need to know that you're either into, or not into, that kind of tech dialogue. Are you? I can do it, but other people do it much better than me.

NK: I'd rather not. I do think our ability to subvert is closely connected to the earlier discussion about our ability to communicate unselfconsciously—how do we "subvert" if we can barely have a direct conversation without all the disclaimers, distance, and adornment?

I've done some writing about the effects of technology on the building of mass movements. I'm not into the sci-fi stuff but on the lower-tech end, there is no doubt that the movements against corporate power that I've been a part of were dramatically shaped by e-mail and the Web. But now these movements are pushing up against the limits of the technologies. They have helped start millions of discussions around the world but they are failing us when it comes to deepening those discussions, and moving from complaint and protest to the building of alternatives.

What's your take on this? It feels pointless and fogeyish to bemoan our shortening attention spans, but more and more I feel like the discussion is central to our democratic crisis. So much is riding on our inability to concentrate or remember—look at what George Bush is getting away with.

DC: To me, I remember working at and with *Wired* magazine back in 1993 and 1994, and how fresh and new the world seemed—imagine sending letters instantly across the planet! It felt revolutionary, and it was, but it all quickly became about establishing a LAN between Marketing and Human Resources, and about finding an e-solution to all of your problems. Have you found an e-solution lately, Naomi?

NK: No, but I'm seriously considering the ultimate e-solution: canceling my e-mail account. As a research tool, it's amazing, but it screws my writing because it's always easier to be sidetracked into one of the hundreds of e-mail conversations I'm supposed to be maintaining. How do you deal with it?

DC: I see it as a phone with twenty hold buttons. As long as I take folic acid every day, I ought to be able to handle it all. My father's convinced it's the end of Alzheimer's.

NK: But how do you keep those expectations from destroying your need as a writer to concentrate deeply, or your ability to fully experience the physical location in which you find yourself, at home or on the road?

DC: I think it's because I came to writing from art school,

where everything is permitted, as opposed to university, where nothing is permitted. Imagine if art schools in 2003 only taught still-life painting and the carving of marble busts—and yet that's what most university English programs are doing with words. So from the art school paradigm, the world is much richer to me in terms of how I can look at it and use it as one great big cosmic art supply. In any event, hotels and airports are like home to me in some ways—in a Pico Ayer sense of the word. I don't sleep in the garage, but it's still part of the house.

NK: But you do care about place and where you live, so what's the secret?

DC: Well, at the moment there's no secret at all. My brain is deep-fried from eight weeks of touring, I haven't had three cohesive sentences to string together on paper in all those weeks, and even once the touring stops, it'll take two weeks for my brain to reach homeostasis. I'm fucked. I have no discipline, really. All I know is that unless I'm surrounded by plant life and birds that I recognize, a certain kind of temperature and sky, nothing is going to happen.

NK: Wait a minute Doug, you never talked about the future of subversion.

DC: Well, look at my mother, who's sixty-seven, and who now lives on the Internet. She used to consider herself center-right-wing, and now she's disgusted with all forms of politics. In the absence of any cohesive political template, she vacillates between charismatics and conspiracy theories. The Internet exposes all forms of shortcomings, yet prohibits the creation of myth. In Ottawa last summer I met a guy at a literary festival who honestly believed the U.S. government planned the 9/11 attacks to make Islam look bad. I was so shocked I could barely speak—that almost never happens to me—and yet he'd read about it online that day and I think he might still believe it now. How can politics work in this sort of universe? In the end, it may all boil down to aura and telegenics. Is your aura powerful enough to obliterate the Polaroids your buddies took during that weekend skiing? Or what about those mash notes you sent your supervisor in 1996? Google, please. Somehow, no matter how cool and detached our technologies make us, sooner or later we're all *tricoteuses*, knitting by the guillotine basket, waiting for the next head to fall. As a detached consumer material rational culture we peaked around 1974. It's been an ugly, embarrassing slide ever since.

NK: It's true, we are devolving.

DC: The only tenable viewpoints of the present I've been able to find come from Eric Hobsbawm, a British intellectual who wrote exclusively from a Marxist stance. While my background is utterly nondoctrinaire, I have noted that once Marxism became a historical novelty, it oddly became genuinely relevant.

Marxism is a structured ideology based on the creation of wealth, the nature of "ownership," and the links of wealth to collective social welfare. It remains eerily precise in decodifying the shifting matrices of capital that define our era. This, in spite of 1989, September 11, 2001, and, as this is a fashion magazine, the intract-ability of acid-wash denim on the former East German style consciousness.

NK: Marx was a brilliant diagnostician. It's his prescriptions that need some work.

DC: Naomi, quickly, what is the statistical probability that someone reading whatever it is we're discussing here, will emerge from it in some way transformed or even radicalized?

NK: 4.5 percent. You?

DC: Maybe 1.5 percent. But it's still more than zero percent. Do you see a certain section of the social pie chart as being "post-radicalizable"? An awful word, and one I've just coined badly. But you catch my drift. Is there a definable, subjectively defined hunk of society whose minds are not fully made up and might be open to voluntary and cathartic social change?

NK: I suspect that there are many people who can't be radicalized by arguments or facts. Having said this, anyone on Earth can be radicalized by things that happen directly to them. I've spent the past year in Argentina making a documentary that looks at how the total economic meltdown in one country forced people to do something we almost never do: change. Everywhere you look, people are openly altering how they think, how they relate to their neighbors. It was amazingly beautiful to witness, but it does seem to require losing a hell of a lot before that happens.

DC: I must see this documentary.

NK: Sadly, I think a lot of this is about self-interest—comfort breeds stasis. Progressives in the United States often try to deal with this by trying to "wake up" the population by hurling alarming facts at them and making them feel guilty about their cars and hamburgers. But my experience is that guilt doesn't last long as a motivator. We need a way of talking about change that questions not just why we are comfortable when so many people aren't but also whether we are as comfortable as we think we are. When Arundhati Roy, the novelist, visits the United States, she doesn't try to make Americans feel guilty, she tries to get them to see that maybe their wonderful way of life isn't as wonderful as their politicians keep telling them that it is. For instance, she describes the American dream as "the right to live alone in your house with your washing machine" and she tells her audiences about what they are missing in countries that have a richer sense of community. Too often we think of "radicalizing" as getting people to give up their self-interest, instead of helping them to see their self-interest in radically different terms, and to see the pleasures of living differently. The biggest obstacle to "the future of subversion" is that we no longer understand how change is supposed to happen.

DC: Ooohhhh . . . Good call.

NK: All of the traditional structures that used to make it easy to organize into political movements have broken down—the huge workplace, the tight-knit community, religion. So just because you have been "radicalized" intellectually doesn't mean you have any real idea about how to turn that radicalism into change.

In *Hey Nostradamus!* you write about one of the ways that people respond to cultural flux: retreating into highly structured rules-based religion. You seem to be saying that it's less about the comfort of faith than the comfort of the rules themselves, a system you can win if you play it right.

DC: For some people, yes. It can be very depressing or very uplifting to see in play.

NK: It seems to me that that's what all fundamentalisms offer, whether it's Wall Street, the Taliban, or Stalin.

DC: Or journalism school. Or Miss America.

NK: So we are in this strange moment where small groups of highly organized fundamentalists are changing the world for us, and most of us are just watching it happen because we don't have their faith in rules. Is this the real "clash of civilizations"? Between fundamentalists and everyone else?

DC: You have to be a very desperate person to trust a rules system unconditionally, yet it seems to be the only way to send a signal to the uncommitted. Look at poor Chile. The middle classes became almost drunk after the election of Salvador Allende. They thought that they could have this peaceful Oz-like society without paying some kind of huge fee. While they were busy congratulating themselves, in came the goon squads. Chile is scary to me, because in so many ways, Canada is in the same boat. Before we get too high on ourselves or our decriminalized pot, or our social leniency, let's not forget the Pinochet lesson.

NK: Doug, we're running out of space here. Quickly, since we're in *BlackBook*, is there such a thing as a fashion or design fundamentalist?

DC: Well, there's the Gap. They became really huge in the nineties because everyone bought their simple, unlabeled clothing but then suddenly everyone realized they had enough basics, so now the Gap is suffering because everyone has "basics fatigue." People want boutique items for made-in-China prices. And then there's the utopian twentieth-century designers like the Eamses who made furniture for the everyman, but, of course, everypeople hated the stuff and only rich, educated, snobby people buy it and worship it. That might be the fate of any ideology worth isolating:

Isolate it, and then sell it back to itself and then find something new. And if nothing else, you can always make up meaningless slogans that sound good but have no calories: "Left is the new center"; "The right is the new left." Facetious drivel. It's like fridge-magnet poetry politics.

NK: Or you can dress up fashion models like Che Guevera and try to talk about Marxism in *BlackBook*. Hey, Doug, I think we're part of the problem! Yikes.

If It Makes You Think, Is It Fashion?

GLENN O'BRIEN

I've got a weird condition called future nostalgia. I long for the good old days when the future was cool. Back then the future was visions of better days ahead: modern living through science, clean lines, simplicity, harmony, proportion, and automated ease. Today the future is a monster movie: *Alien vs. Predator.* Either way, we lose. It's postmodernism, a collision of styles as a high-concept joke.

But I want to go back to modernism, that old-fashioned idea of the future. I want to live in a Neutra House and drive an Avanti and wear a Nehru suit and drink Gibsons with the wife dressed in Gernreich and listen to Miles Davis "In a Silent Way" or frug to the Ventures, because nobody's done anything better. We peaked too soon. Today's future isn't worth going to. We've lost our optimism and imagination. Today's concept of "superior aliens" looks like weasel fetuses. In 1951 aliens looked like

Michael Rennie, totally fly guys, genuine superior beings. We had a future then, but now it's global warming, jihad, and melanoma. As if things could only get worse. I look at architect Frank Gehry's downtown Guggenheim design and pinch myself hoping it's just a bad dream.

Frank Lloyd Wright looked marvelous, even when he was an old man, like he was when he built the Guggenheim Museum: wearing a well-tailored suit, a cool Cab Calloway hat, a mystical beaded scarf, a bohemian fly-away bow tie. He was a visionary artist and he had no use for fashion. He said, "Fashion exists for commercial purposes only. The fashionable thing is valueless to culture."

I'll give you a minute to walk around the room, look out the window, look in the mirror and think about that one.

Everybody in New York and Los Angeles talks about fashion. Our culture has gone fashion crazy. People watch fashion shows on TV. They talk about what's in and laugh at what's out. But nobody ever talks about what fashion is.

To Louis XIV fashion wasn't commerce, it was politics. By setting an impossible standard of competition through fashion follies he virtually imprisoned the nobility of France in the exquisite one-upmanship of court life, exhausting their financial means, consolidating power in the throne, and making his nation a world power. Of course for the nobles it was simply keeping up with Le Joneses.

But what function does fashion serve today? I think fashion is witchcraft, just like it was in the twelfth century. It's a very good way to get the peasants' attention and keep them squabbling among themselves, preening, and posturing. It's also one of our most effective distractions from political reality. An organized form of narcissism, fashion distracts the population from economics, ecology, and "current events." Who needs to worry about the Sudan when we've got John Galliano?

Fashion is not the only thing we've got to keep democracy from working. There's drugs, sports, and reality TV, Paris Hilton, Donald Trump, Martha Stewart, and Scott Peterson. But fashion is one of the most efficient distractions for the bourgeoisie intent on moving on up to the East Side. In recent years fashion has even managed to semi-destroy the art world by infiltrating and co-opting it. The art world has ceded recognition to fashion designers who are arty, while artists have gotten involved in fashion. Take Vanessa Beecroft. Please!

So basically fashion is sports for women, an opiate of the leisure class. But could it be something more significant? Well, maybe fashion—the things we put on our backs to signify our "individuality" and specialness—could be a form of white magic. Maybe instead of being a distraction from harsh realities it could be a way of dealing with them. Maybe instead of being a smoke screen fashion could be smoke signals. If you can't get the truth on TV or in the newspaper, maybe you can get it on a T-shirt. Not likely, but possible.

In my closet I have a "Fuck Bush" T-shirt and one that says "My Dick Would Make a Better Vice President." Of course, I'm not going to pack them in my luggage next time I fly to the coast. Maybe I could get my vintage "Eat the Rich" tee through Homeland Security without getting put on the "no-fly" list with Teddy Kennedy, but do I want to risk it? But I think this has potential. Fashion can be dangerous. That's why we have to take off our shoes at the airport. But how could we make it more dangerous, make it revolutionary? How could we make it positive-political instead of negative-political. I think the answer is making fashion cultural again.

Before fashion became commerce, clothing was cultural and ceremonial. It created a form. Formality created form. People had good form or bad form. Good form connected people to their culture, to their roots, to the path of true social progress. White tie was ceremonial. Black tie was ceremonial. The cocktail dress and the twin set and even the miniskirt were ceremonial. Fashion was an integral part of ceremony, cultural practice, ritual. Putting on clothes made people feel secure and connected.

Today fashion designers sometimes hint at ritual. Sometimes they create clothes that verge on being cultural. It happens among the few who practice art in their fashion work, designers like Jean Paul Gaultier. He so admired the ritual of Hasidic dress he put it into his collection. He was reviled and attacked. Why? Was he making fun of the Hasidim? Hardly. It was even more dangerous. He was making us think about what clothing means.

What does Hasidic clothing mean? What does Amish clothing mean? Is it retro? Is it about self-denial or group identity? Is it about separation or unity? Is it anti-future, anti-fashion? Is it a form of correction (like say a stock market crash)? Is it about getting back to a simpler, more meaningful life?

Calvin Klein did Amish in the nineties. So did Donna Karan. Is a Helmut Lang suit of today very different in spirit from Amish-wear? What about the veil? Is the burka fashion or is it political? Designer Hussein Chalayan showed a veiled woman in various states of dress, from mini to bottomless. If it makes you think, is it still fashion?

I like some of the signs I see on the runway. I like Imitation of Christ showing a collection of ethereal goddess dresses and Greek-style white tunics that look like what Bacchae girls might wear before going out on a frenzy to tear a man to pieces with their fingers. I like Hussein Chalayan showing clothes that look like folkloric costumes from the Himalayas. He seems to understand that nobody looks better than an Inca or Tibetan or Masai or Nuba wearing what is traditional. Unless of course it's a woman in a little black dress or a man in white tie. But we've been throwing out our own cultural tradition for a half-century. We've been killing our own ritual. Look at a photo of businessmen fifty years ago. We're going casual.

Do you know why? Is it because the rich are getting richer and the top 1 percent own almost everything? So they're afraid anybody wearing a top hat and spats might get killed? Is Bill Gates's sweater and jeans the equivalent of the Mao suit, the one look for the masses? What other possible explanation is there for $1,000 jeans and $500 sneakers? The new class differentiation is economic camouflage, how to look rich in code.

Meanwhile working men are in crisis over casual dress. When the workplace called for suits they knew what to do. They wore what was expected. Now that they have been "set free" they are confused. In *Sex and Suits* Anne Hollander writes: "We have largely reconceived dress as personal not social theater, partly out of the modishness of the anti-fashion posture. Outward pressure to conformity is now perceived as an infringement of personal liberty. . . . Currently accepted attitudes discourage the idea of a harmonious public picture, suggesting instead that each of us should make a satisfactory single image of our individual figure without consideration for what the larger group will do."

The result is a mass crisis of identity and confidence. The public is a mess and the individual longs for his lost uniform. The frightening thing is that someone may come along with one as snappy as the seductive threads of the Weimar SS. But what was wrong with "the way we were"? I remember the old days and how great men looked when everyone in the room wore the same black tux. We still had our different lapels, bow ties, and cummerbunds, and beyond that we had our faces, and somehow people all came together. But now we have total freedom. Freedom to walk down the street with our ass cracks showing. Freedom to arrive at a gala in underwear. Was it worth it?

There's a great Web store called Plainly Dressed. They sell "plain, modest, Christian clothing" for a mainly Amish and Mennonite clientele. It's fabulous. The clothing is made to order, comes in a variety of fabrics and linings, and looks like Comme des Garçons or Helmut Lang. And it's not fashion. It's anti-fashion. It's simple and unchanging. It's cultural. It's ritual.

Ritual is about finding meaning in the things we do over and over again. Perhaps there's still something magic in it, even for post-postmoderns like us. Something that could get us away from the nightmares on our screens that have replaced culture.

When you get dressed, think about what it means. When you have a meal think about what that means. Once gods oversaw the little rituals, giving meaning to the smallest human actions, the ones we repeat endlessly. I think paying attention to what we're doing and not pretending we're someone we're not could lead us back to culture, back to a life filled with the riches of meaning.

I always remember what Andy Warhol said: "The best look is a good plain look." That's one way to get your face back.

Harold and Maude Is Forever

EMMA FORREST

I remember being twenty-one and watching *Harold and Maude* with a writer who kept grabbing my ass. "You're like dessert," he whispered in my ear as Harold gave Maude the locket inscribed "Harold loves Maude," and I thought, "Hey, would you squeeze the profiteroles?" As Maude throws the locket into the sea—"so I'll always know where it is!"—he suggested we retire to the bedroom. It made me furious. He had no notion of the gift I was opening up to him, a real window into my soul. *Harold and Maude* for Christ's sake: one of the pop-culture cornerstones that make up my id. I could have played him *Darkness on the Edge of Town* by Bruce Springsteen, loaned him the translated *Novel with Cocaine* by M. Ageyev, taken him to see *Ophelia Drowning*, which, as a little girl at the Tate Gallery, I stood before, transfixed.

Some people fear that they are no more than the sum of their cultural reference points: the books read, films seen, the posters on the walls, and records on rotation. I am happy to admit this. What then remains, for a vampire of pop culture when love is over? What of the books loaned, the records recommended? What gets passed to the next lover, what gets sold for cash at Rebel Rebel? When a relationship ends, I sell none of it, filing it all away for future reference, marveling at how the most dreadful person can turn you on to the most beautiful music or film. These gifts, given in ego—this is me, this is me, have some more of me—are like transferable tattoos. These books and videos, they are stronger than those ephemeral fights, even the ephemeral fucking.

Years after the writer, I was with a man younger than me, Harold's age, twenty-one, the age I had been, and I wanted him to see the film with me before we parted. I sat next to him and watched his face as he watched. We did break up that week, as I sensed we would, and as sad as I was, I was never sorry that I had introduced him to that film. He was special enough and sensitive enough. He understood what I was giving him. When the Dalai Lama dies a new one is born the same day. He became, in my head, the Dalai Harold. It has been two years since it ended with the Dalai Harold. He gave me a lot of music, turning up on my doorstep flushed with excitement, carrying an Other Music bag. For the first three months after the breakup I kept the CDs he gave me hidden in a cupboard, then moved them, like a premature baby, first to the nursery and then "home," the shelves above my desk: Wilco's *Yankee Hotel Foxtrot*. *Point* by Cornelius. *My Life in the Bush of Ghosts* by David Byrne and Brian Eno.

It amazed me, as it always had, that there could be so much out there I had neither heard nor heard of before my love introduced me to it. It can feel frightening at first—if there are so many records I didn't know about, perhaps there are whole worlds out there too—yet, when love is over, it becomes comforting. Perhaps there are whole worlds out there.

Once upon a time I made the world's most halfhearted attempt to kill myself over a man: eight aspirin and a long sleep. When I woke up, my friend David, who had long been in love with me, took me to the Hard Rock Café, where he asked that we sit under the gold record for *Darkness on the Edge of Town*; thus I saw it before I ever heard it. David was a handsome Welshman, coarse black hair and language. "Hey," he said, as the aspirin kicked around my stomach, "You look like Elizabeth Taylor if she'd just been fucked by Richard Burton." All Welsh men are in love with Elizabeth Taylor and so, in a double whammy of affection, he introduced me to both Bruce and Liz, the archetypes of manhood and femininity. He'd come to my house and we'd lie in bed and watch Springsteen concert films and he'd sigh, "I love you, Bruce!" then turn to me in his Welshness: "Not in a gay way. I just want to hug him." The man, the one I tried to kill myself for, I remember very little of him other than he looked like a vampire that just woke up.

David and I were going to take a road trip, listening to Springsteen on repeat, but we ended up taking the trips alone. I have no idea where he is now, but *Darkness on the Edge of Town* still makes frustration and sorrow turn, in my mouth, to a fine wine, swirled, enjoyed, wallowed in. And on the cover of the record, which hangs in my bedroom, Bruce looks, with his dark curly hair and white v-neck t-shirt, like David.

It feels very different when the breakup is acrimonious. What I would give—a Shylock's lump of flesh—to take back having played *Darkness on the Edge of Town* to that fool who squirmed during *Harold and Maude.* I was ashamed to return David's calls for a long time because I had disgraced our album. That's how we drifted apart.

I ended up drifting into the most handsome man I had ever seen, a divorced father of an equally gorgeous five-year-old boy. On a drive between Los Angeles and San Diego I played him *Thirteen* by Blur. "White people's music," he sneered at first— Damon Albarn's upturned nose a world away, the dreams of young Britain resting on Albarn's slender shoulders, the dreams of our own future here in the car. And when I left him, he told me he listened to it over and over again, longing shot into his veins.

I found myself back in touch with Dalai Harold, who as sweet as he ever was, told me that he had passed *Harold and Maude* on to other people. "The value of those things you gave to me," he said, voice deeper than I remembered, "maintained after things fell apart. I've kept them in my life because of you, but also because of their own value. I'm sure it's all wrapped up together."

These are the three most important men I've had in my life, although I was not with any of them the longest (Dalai Harold a month, the Welsh Bruce a recurring theme for a year and a half, the father eleven months and three weeks). When someone you love dies, it is common to take on some of their traits in order to keep them alive. The loss of love is like mourning, instead of tics you keep the records, books, movies.

The father, who, if such things exist, was the love of my life, gave me nothing. No books, no records, although he always promised to. I had no cultural help. All I had was him. I could not understand it when it ended. There was no Tom Waits to help me, no Milan Kundera, no unsung Altman movie. Well, there's one thing: one night when we were about to watch *Harold and Maude* he ran out to pick up two tubs of Tasti D-Lite at the frozen yogurt store that I had passed a hundred times but never entered. "You've never had a Tasti D-Lite?" he gasped. When the mother of his child was pregnant she became addicted to the stuff. He did midnight runs for her and now he was doing them for me, who was trying very hard not to get pregnant but still grateful for frozen yogurt in August. He brought it back and we watched *Harold and Maude*, at the end of which he turned to me and said, "I want to make love to you when you're eighty." He had put his finger on my fixation with the movie, which is quite simply: "Will you still love me tomorrow?"

The last night we spent together he walked me from one branch of Tasti D-Lite to another, downing three cups in one hour. In his frozen frenzy he was painting himself as a man who consumes, who takes what he wants when he wants it, who throws caution to the wind. He is none of these things. But here, in a tiny gesture, he offered a vision of how our relationship could have been.

Movies, books, and records, fixed, pinned like butterflies, unchanging and serene, are never going to melt. Thinking of him I take just a few licks of a Tasti D-Lite—it is enough, it is too much—and then throw it in the trash. Harold loves Maude. There. So I'll always know where it is.

The Angriest
Book Club in America

BRUNO MADDOX

I have been warned. The Underground Literary Alliance—
known for gate-crashing book readings in Manhattan
and heckling the authors to explain the relevance of their
self-absorbed, oh-so-clever postmodern novels to ordinary
people trying to make ends meet in George W. Bush's America—
has explicitly sent word that I am to expect "trouble" when I
come to interview them in Philadelphia, where they are based.
The ULA apparently has Googled me, decided that I—like a
lot of people—embody everything that's wrong with the modern publishing industry, and they are therefore planning some
sort of "ambush." This makes me apprehensive. Frankly, the
whole thing is shaping up a bit too Daniel Pearl for my
tastes—though I suppose I should be grateful I don't have a
pregnant wife. Man. Talk about irony. I was just thinking how
much I wanted one.

Sure enough, on a bright but overcast Pennsylvania lunchtime I step lightly into the sticky gloom of a bar called Dirty Frank's and find myself greeted with a volley of abuse.

"Is this the writer?" comes a voice. "He looks like a fucking writer."

(Conflict is the soul of a strong narrative, and I have been instructed by the editors of this magazine to dress as much like a prancing Manhattan aesthete as possible. Above a pair of veal-toned Cole Haan loafers I am in: a light fawn suit, beltless, and a particularly fruity plum and lavender shirt with twinkly cuff links.)

"Jesus Christ," exclaims some other person. "Check this guy out."

And it begins.

Most people—meaning most of the very small group of people who give a shit—attribute the Death of the Novel to vast cultural forces beyond the control of mere mortals. If today's best-seller lists are glutted with artless formulaic blockbusters, when forty years ago it was wall-to-wall Norman Mailer and John Updike . . . well, hey. It's probably television's fault, or movies, or the collapse of the school system. . . . Something like that, anyway.

To a Detroit freight-forwarding clerk named Karl "King" Wenclas, however, recuperating in 1998 from a near-fatal apartment fire, the Death of the Novel was no accident. In the mid-1980s, after writing his own novel and having it rejected, Wenclas had stumbled across the world of literary "zines" and underground presses, where it became increasingly clear to him that the best American writing was being ignored by Big Publishing. The only novels that ever seemed to get published were effete, pointlessly "clever" verbal exercises about the exploits of upper-class, Ivy-educated pansies walking around Manhattan and making witty remarks.

That the authors of these novels were also upper-class, Ivy-educated, martini-sipping New York pansies struck Wenclas as no coincidence. These people clearly had hijacked the book industry, and downgraded the Novel from a once-powerful instrument of social change to a stress-relieving plaything for the urban bourgeoisie. No wonder mainstream America had come to prefer television and Mary Higgins Clark. The nation did still have great writers, Karl knew, because he'd read them, think-outside-the-box types with names such as Wild Bill Blackolive and Crazy Carl Robinson, but because they didn't go to Brown and weren't making the nightly scene at Da Silvano's their only hope of getting published was to go to Kinko's and talk to the man in the stripy shirt.

Lying there on his sickbed, between episodes of reflective delerium à la *The English Patient* (during one of which he had a vision of moving to Philadelphia), Karl Wenclas decided that enough was enough. Life was passing him by and it was time to make an impact.

His first step was to a distribute among his zine-head friends a pamphlet-of-intent titled "How to Start a Literary Movement."

And then, by golly, he started one.

Two years later, if Karl Wenclas didn't exactly have the Manhattan literary world cowering in the palm of his hand, he was at least in a position to tap it on the shoulder and have it turn and say, "Yes, Karl; what is it?" The ULA's inaugural action—a petition protesting a $35,000 Guggenheim grant to wealthy novelist Rick Moody of *The Ice Storm* acclaim—had gotten a lot of play in the press. More protests had followed, more attention, and by 2002 as big a name as Jonathan *The Corrections* Franzen was writing to Wenclas personally to defend his acceptance of a $20,000 grant from the NEA. When the ULA challenged George Plimpton of *The Paris Review* to debate them on literature, Plimpton actually showed up. The ULA was on the map. For twenty-three rough-and-ready underground writers and one revitalized freight-forwarding clerk, things were going better than they could have dreamed.

However, it was around this time that the ULA started doing their own showing-up. They started showing up at readings by authors they considered insufficiently "real" and disrupting the proceedings. Records of these events are preserved, like cave-paintings, amid screeds against Dave Eggers and a whole sheaf of manifestos, on the ULA's website, www.literaryrevolution.com. Some excerpts:

> The ULA crashed an effete, boring reading given at KGB in NYC by a boring writer and made some noise and shouted "Is this what literature is about?". . . They challenged the crowd to throw them out; the bouncers obliged. Alcohol was involved.

> Emotions were very stirred. Karl ranted out loud: "Literature has become something stuck on a dusty shelf in a library!" The literary-reading attendees groaned. An older gent in an urban cowboy hat strongly suggested that Karl shut up. "Why don't

you make me?" challenged the King. The old man arose. Karl led him toward the door, where the older man then balked and failed to cross the line into the danger zone where the King was poised.

People were confused. The ULA's raids seemed like an odd piece of policy for a group that was making such headway with just a fax machine and the moral highground. Among the bewildered was novelist Thomas Beller. He and Wenclas had been enjoying a robust but civilized correspondence about the editorial policy of Beller's literary journal *Open City* when, just this past January, the ULA stormed an *Open City* event at the Housing Works and ended up scuffling with Beller on the sidewalk. From Karl's lurid, online account of the incident:

> I could've punched him out—he would've made a very large human heavy punching bag; he acted ready to fight, though he scarcely knew how, and his eyes were dazed and spinning and empty and he said from the fog of his brain, as if I were the problem, when he'd been the asshole, "I thought you were my friend!"

It is now late afternoon in Philadelphia, where the weather has worsened, and although perhaps I am no closer to an understanding of the ULA and its paradoxes, I too am beginning to think that Karl "King" Wenclas is my friend. Wenclas, who looks like an exact cross between Chris Cooper's character in *Adaptation* and someone with a full set of teeth, would seem to be the nicest guy in the world. In the company of two apparently legendary underground poets, Frank Walsh and Michael "Mad Dog" Grover, the King and I have drunk a phenomenal quantity of alcohol and had what can only be described as a damn good time. Far from "ambushing" me, the Underground Literary Alliance—after, sure, a few edgy, ice-breaking compliments on my metropolitan finery—have literally catered to my every whim. I demanded to sample an authentic Philadelphia cheese steak and they drove me to get one. I even, half-jokingly, requested a woman, and after a few phone calls, they produced Natalie C. Felix, a hugely attractive twenty-two-year-old soon-to-be-apparently-legendary blond poet.

In fact, it seems the only thing I can't get Karl to do is bad-mouth the literary establishment with any kind of sincerity or conviction. In trying to clarify the ULA's position on a few minor points—what disqualifies *The Corrections* as one of the ULA's beloved Great Social Novels?; what makes literary journals like Tom Beller's *Open City*, Dave Eggers's *McSweeney's* so despicably different from the ULA's own literary zine, *Slush Pile*—I have managed to elicit an awful lot of shrugging, as well as a fairly stunning series of concessions:

"Actually, I like a lot of what Dave [Eggers] does; I just think he could do more";

"Jonathan Franzen's okay; he's probably the novel's best hope right now";

George Plimpton, more the inventor of New York literary culture than mere embodiment, Wenclas finds "very impressive, a very impressive guy."

And sure, on balance, *Open City* and *McSweeney's* are *"a good thing,"* and even Tom Beller *"is more of a friend than an enemy."*

That's all I can get out of him. As we are draining what must surely be our final round of drinks at a bar in the train station—where the ULA has very kindly driven me—I gently point out to Karl that he has, over the course of the afternoon, expressed admiration and even solidarity with just about every name on the ULA's list of enemies.

Wenclas drops his eyes, says softly, "Look. We don't hate anyone. We're just trying to get some attention for our writers. That's all."

It is time for me to go.

There are hugs.

One of the truer truisms about the twentieth century is that it saw "Why am I here?" replaced with "Why aren't I famous?" as the big existential question plaguing all thinking organisms. Flipping through the ULA's (unreadable) *Slush Pile* on the train back to Manhattan I'm finding it hard to shake a mounting suspicion that for all its activist bluster, the fundamental purpose of an organization like the ULA is to provide its members with a workable answer to that question. That answer being:

(a) Dude, you are famous. You're a legendary figure, Crazy John Doe, one of America's greatest living writers. It's just that you're an underground literary figure, and that's only

(b) Because you're too good at writing. Dude, your work's too powerful. The Man can't let it be published because he knows it would bring down the whole system. He won't publish you because he doesn't dare.

And I find myself wondering if perhaps Karl didn't think it would be harder to get the literary world's attention than it was. If publishing types had only ignored the ULA's protests with the same consistency that they rejected its manuscripts, the ULA-ers could have kept on pretending that they were the victims of simple prejudice, rather than their own abysmal prose. But no, people paid attention. And that spoiled everything. If your entire sense of self rests on the idea of being a Barbarian at the Gate, then all of a sudden the gate opens up and there's George Plimpton in a blazer beckoning you in . . . well, you've got a problem. Now you're a barbarian at a cocktail party. You don't know anyone. Your hair looks like shit. You're the only person carrying a cudgel. It's awkward. And you have a difficult choice to make: Either prove you belong inside the gate; whip a man-uscript out of your bearskin tunic and show these toffs that you can hold your own, that you're just as good as they are. Or, if you privately know that the manuscript in your tunic just isn't any good, despite all the nice things your fellow barbarians said about it around the campfire, then your only option is the one Karl and his friends ended up going for—cause a drunken ruckus and try to get yourself thrown out, back out beyond the gate, where deep down you know you belong.

I find the whole thing sad, and it is with mixed emotions that I de-train unsteadily into the splendor of a Saturday evening in Manhattan. That the Underground Literary Alliance should be so right about so much, yet lack the maturity or self-belief to actually make a difference, strikes me as a minor tragedy. A five-figure grant going to a writer who wouldn't need a day job any-way really doesn't make sense, when you think about it. And that so many of the brightest, most creative Americans spend so much time arranging words in decorative, meaningless patterns, rather than using those talents to change the world, really does seem a shame . . . although it would appear, as I am delighted to report to several writer friends over martinis at the Soho Grand, that we are probably safe to keep doing it for at least a little while longer.

Clink!

More than forty years after coming to national attention with her first novel, *Run River*, Joan Didion's spare, unblinkered prose continues to shock and awe new generations of readers. Though her essay collections, *Slouching Towards Bethlehem* and *The White Album* remain her most celebrated works, her nuanced political analyses for the *New York Review of Books* continue to provide a cold blast of reality in these politically dishonest times.

Like Didion's essays in the 1960s, Meghan Daum's candescent essay collection, *My Misspent Youth*, explores the way we live now through the prism of personal experience: The title essay—a rage against the betrayal of dreams—acutely captures the sense of disillusion that has long been a Didion staple. Now living in Los Angeles, Daum is also the author of *The Quality of Life Report*. The two writers met in Didion's New York apartment for a conversation on identity, geography, and *Vogue*.

BlackBook: Both of you have written essays about falling out of love with New York—Joan in "Goodbye to All That," and Meghan in "My Misspent Youth." Were you writing about New York or yourselves?

Joan Didion: I think certainly in Meghan's case, but in my case too, falling out of love with New York is a situation of not having enough money [*laughs*]. I think that's why people fall out of love with New York at a certain point. If you have enough money, it gets better and better.

Meghan Daum: One of Joan's most memorable lines, for me, in "Goodbye to All That" was that New York was a city for the very rich and the very young.

JD: Well, we moved from here to Los Angeles in 1964, and it was totally amazing to me, the sense of luxury. We rented a house on the ocean, we had forty acres of oceanfront, we had three bedrooms and three bathrooms and rose gardens and artichoke gardens, and all of this was taken care of, and we were paying four hundred dollars a month. We were going to go out there for six months, and then we kept staying on, but it was so much easier to live on less.

MD: That's astonishing to me. Was there something about the economics of that city at the time? It seems remarkable.

JD: It was remarkable, but to get from Beverly Hills to our house you had to get on the San Diego freeway, go past all the refineries, and then all the way out to the ocean. So it was a hard house to rent, because it was so far from town. They were asking eight hundred dollars a month and I said we couldn't possibly afford eight hundred dollars a month, but maybe we could afford four hundred dollars, and they took us.

BlackBook: Your feelings about New York—the sense of feeling very, very young here. Is it more of an idea than a reality? Was it something you started seeing through?

MD: I had a real anger that I couldn't make it work—I think a lot of my work comes out of an anger, and that's where the urgency to write the piece comes from.

JD: Who were you working for?

MD: I worked at *Allure*, which is part of Condé Nast, and I guess we're all naive about our notions of New York, or anywhere when we're growing up, and I had this set of cultural icons that I associated with New York. But after being there for a while and seeing that I was doing everything I could, and actually making pretty decent money and *still* not able to make it, I was furious, and angry—particularly during the nineties and the whole boom that occurred—that I had been left out of it, but more that New York was a prohibitively expensive place for the people who had made it what it was: the creative people and the intellectuals and the artists.

JD: For me there was some kind of cognitive dissonance between the way I lived and the place I was working. I was working for *Vogue*, and people there really did not have a clear understanding of what it was to be making forty-five or fifty dollars a week, which is what I started at. I can remember asking if someone could get me a discount on a Polo coat, because I needed a winter coat, and she said, "Oh sweetie, a Polo coat is all wrong for you, put yourself in Hattie Carnegie's hands, she does wonderful things for small people." Put yourself in Hattie Carnegie's hands! So I kept feeling poorer even than I was.

MD: I was mistaken for a messenger one time, walking into Three Hundred Fifty Madison, because I was so bedraggled and poorly dressed. They stopped me at the desk and told me to take the freight elevator, and I said, "I'm an assistant."

I'm really curious to talk to you about this, because that was 1992, and it was the closest I felt I could come to a literary, glamorous job. I knew nothing about fashion. I had no interest in it—I pronounced *Versace* as Versayce—but it's interesting how the fashion world is intrinsically linked to being a writer for women.

JD: Yeah, in a certain way it was a way in. *Vogue*, at least, had a features department, so we had all these semi-literary projects going on.

MD: I wondered about that. Was that your very first job?

JD: I got the Prix de Paris, so I got a job out of college, but I wasn't immediately put in the features department—basically, all I did for a about a year was read back issues, and then I started working in the promotional department, and in order to get into the features department I actually had to quit, and then they said they would move me to the features department.

MD: This was in the fifties?

JD: I went there in the fall of 1956 and I stayed there until late 1963.

MD: I'm really curious about what allowed for it to be a time in which a women's magazine or fashion magazine had more intellectual merit.

JD: Well, *Harper's Bazaar* was one of the big fiction outlets, and *Mademoiselle* was, too.

MD: Right, Sylvia Plath wrote for *Mademoiselle*.

JD: Yes, and Margarita Smith, who was Carson McCullers's sister, was the fiction editor.

MD: So when did the change happen? When did the publications lose their intellectual credibility, so to speak?

JD: Well, I think there are still things in these magazines, but it's harder to find them because of the layout—the deliberate mingling of advertising with editorial makes it very difficult to present material in a way that you take seriously. At that time, you'd pick up a copy of *Vogue* or *Harper's Bazaar*, and there were X pages of advertising—

many, many pages—but they were all discreet: You had an advertising section, then an introductory page, and then you went into the well and didn't see advertising again until you got to the end of the book.

It was much more like a family than you would have thought it would be. The personnel director of Condé Nast would stop me in the hall to ask me if I'd called my mother, and if I said, "Not since last Tuesday," she'd say, "Come into my office right now and call her." And they had a nurse, Miss K, who every morning would line up little paper cups of phenobarbitol for you if you came in nervous.

MD: Oh, I wish they hadn't done away with that.

JD: You could take naps in Miss K's office.

MD: It's so interesting because it ties in to this idea I had a long time ago that Seven Sisters Colleges embodied a sensibility that was a direct parallel to the culture of Condé Nast and that somehow, over time, both cultures had been perverted by various cultural forces.

JD: Yeah, the people in charge of Condé Nast saw themselves *in loco parentis*, really. They had all these young children who came to work for them, and they took care of them in a sense.

BlackBook: What would you attribute to the change in that culture?

MD: Maybe cocaine [*both laugh*].

JD: At the time I began working at *Vogue*, there was a very clear understanding that it was not a magazine for very many people. It had two hundred fifty thousand to three hundred fifty thousand subscribers, and then a large pass-along readership, but it was specifically designed as a magazine for not very many people. Once the Newhouses had bought it and settled in, that was no longer the way that the magazine was conceived. It had to build circulation all the time. If you're building circulation all the time you're going to have a different sort of magazine.

BlackBook: Isn't that where we are now, with big conglomerates owning the titles, focused on—

MD: —Well, just reaching the middlebrow and erroneously believing that people want something less intelligent and stupider and more offensive and less interesting than they could take if something else was given to them. There's a Hollywood culture that's about, "Well, we would love to do it this way, but we can't because we've got to appeal to people in Lincoln, Nebraska." Well, I've lived in Lincoln, Nebraska, and I think they would love to read something else.

JD: It's like everybody telling us that out there, in the middle of the country, the places we don't understand were all for the [Iraq] war. Well, they weren't.

BlackBook: It seems that the question of what it means to be American is greater than ever.

JD: Well, I think the question of what it means to be an American was unformed in the back of my mind when I was doing this last book. I kept calling it a book about California, but it wasn't really a book about California; it was a book about how the emptiness and lack of attachments in the western migration in some way doomed that settlement, which is a story of America.

MD: When you came to New York from California, did you feel like New York was the ultimate place, the place where you would stay?

JD: It had to be here, yes, it had to. During my junior and senior years in college, I came as a *Mademoiselle* guest editor—you can see how crazy I was to get out of California that I entered a contest—and the first time I came to New York it was so thrilling to me that I just thought I had to get back here, so I threw myself into the *Vogue* contest and got back here. I never thought I would leave—I couldn't imagine it that time.

MD: And what was the experience like, of being a writer in California? Because there are such specific ideas behind being a writer in New York.

JD: It was great, because nobody knew what you were doing, so there was not a lot of pressure on you. That was one of the things that was driving me nuts in New York. Everybody was talking about—

MD: —Blurbs. It's horrible.

JD: And what their new book was, and any idea you had, had already been sold by someone else. In California, you're totally free of that. Was that kind of pressure one of the reasons you left?

MD: No, you know what it was, really, is that I felt very provincial. This is really hard to describe and sounds very New Agey, which is the opposite of what I mean, if anything, but I just felt there was a piece of myself that was utterly undeveloped.

JD: You hadn't found a role.

MD: I didn't know how to drive, really—for me, New York was infantilizing, and I didn't want to be that person.

JD: That's interesting, because it is [infantilizing] in a lot of ways. I have never driven in New York—I would be afraid to drive in New York.

MD: But you're not going to die, you're just going to bang up your car, and in Los Angeles you could die any time.

JD: There are so many rules that are totally followed in Los Angeles. Everybody knows how to merge, for example. But here would be like driving in Cairo.

MD: Well, there is a Third World quality to it. I considered moving to Los Angeles when I left New York, but I felt it wouldn't be different enough, I wasn't going to accomplish what I needed to accomplish somehow, by doing that. I needed to go into America, because New York is not the United States, it's its own entity. Los

Angeles is certainly more American than New York, but it's still—

JD: —Different.

BlackBook: In "My Misspent Youth," you talk about authenticity in New York—and in *The Quality of Life Report*, your character goes to the Midwest trying to customize her life. Did you find authenticity there, or were you just customizing it again around your ideas of what it should be like?

MD: I grew up primarily in New Jersey, because my father wanted to make his career in New York. But, for various reasons, in my mind anyway, our family seemed very *other* to the people in the community and the town, so in some ways I feel I'm not really from anywhere, and what I now know is that I'll never be from anywhere.

JD: I'm from California, I definitely know that—I still have a California driver's license for example—but it has less power over me than it had. In fact, when I finished *Where I Was From*, for the first time it occurred to me that next time I renewed my license, I would probably have to get a New York license just because my mother had died in the meantime and I don't spend as much time in California.

BlackBook: Was that symbolic for you?

JD: It was a big thing for me. I would never change my driver's license, but I think I might now.

MD: Even though you don't drive here.

JD: Even though I don't drive here.

MD: Isn't that funny—it's like your birth certificate.

***BlackBook*:** Does this increasingly atomized society, with people moving around more freely than ever, lead to a reduced sense of who we are?

JD: Well, I don't know. Even in our experience with everybody moving from place to place and having less sense of being from a national entity, we're seeing this surge of nationalism.

MD: But so rooted in sentimentality, and maybe it's compensating for transience.

JD: For the absence of the real thing.

MD: I really want to get into this question of sentimentality, because when people ask why you are influential to someone like me and a lot of writers—particularly women of my generation—I think it does have to do with your completely unsentimental path in terms of tone. We're so overwhelmed by cheap, oozing sentiment and kitschy emotional content that I wondered if you had ever, in your career, felt burdened by having to have the unpopular take on things, if people would accuse you of being mean—

JD: —Cynical is what they always say.

MD: Well, I just get accused of being mean, and I find that my work has been very polarizing to readers, and it's funny, but in retrospect when "My Misspent Youth" was in *The New Yorker* it made a lot of people very angry.

JD: What was the root of it?

MD: Well, people had a literal read of it, and they thought I was complaining about money. I remember doing a call-in show on [local NPR station] WNYC about the piece, and this caller said, "I'm tired of this whining. Why doesn't she just take a walk in the park, that's free." It's like this inability of American readers to walk and chew gum at the same time. In my mind the piece was an answer to [Edith Wharton's] *The House of Mirth*, about the demise that can occur when fantasies go awry in a city like New York. So I guess I'm just curious about how you coped with that?

JD: I was starting a column for *Life*, and we happened to be in Hawaii, and I had to write my first column introducing myself, and right then the My Lai stuff broke, so I called my editor at *Life* and said I wanted to go out to Vietnam, but he said, "No, some of the guys are going out—you just introduce yourself," and I was so angry that I introduced myself in a very un-*Life*-like way. *Life* at that time had eleven million readers, and I got an awful lot of feedback, a lot of it negative, a lot of it more responsive than I could deal with.

MD: Do you remember what the column was saying?

JD: It's in *The White Album*.

MD: I remember. Deciding whether or not to get divorced? Oh, wow.

JD: Then *Play It As It Lays* came out shortly after, which was read as autobiographical, although it wasn't, and so between *Play It As It Lays*, and that column, I was getting a lot of that. It was kind of a burden, and I was relieved when my whole range started moving toward the political.

MD: Was it conscious?

JD: No. I'd gotten interested while I was doing *A Book of Common Prayer*; then I had started actually following the Vietnam War, which I had ignored for a long time, and then I started writing *Democracy*. So it was all during that period. It started, really, I think, with the Kennedy assassination, but it didn't surface until—

MD: —See that's so interesting, because I'm very self-conscious about how I have not yet found a significant area of inquiry.

JD: I didn't feel that I could. I didn't feel that I had the authority, or the right in some way.

MD: I just feel that I don't have the knowledge. I don't feel I have the historical perspective. I suspect I was in a coma all through college.

JD: I definitely was in a coma. I could quote a lot of English poetry—that's what I did in college—and I could give you the house and garden imagery of a lot of English novels. You could have asked me what the Boer War was and I couldn't have told you.

BlackBook: Isn't the best fiction a kind of social history anyway?

JD: Well, there's an interesting thing. All that great English fiction was social history, but I came to feel that it was impossible to write social history in America because it didn't have a unified audience. There wasn't a universally accepted social norm, so it was much harder to write—you couldn't write as the omniscient narrator.

MD: I want to ask you about that, too. I realized about halfway through writing my first novel that the first person is so limiting, and if there had been a software program to go back and change all the "I"s to "she"s I would have done it. You do a thing like [Philip] Roth often does with Zuckerman—you have a close observer. But, then, how do you get away with them knowing so much? You have to limit yourself.

JD: No, quite early on you say, "Some of what I know, I know from the past, the rest I believe to be true," or some variation on that paragraph.

MD: Really? People will buy that?

JD: It came up for the first time with me in *The Book of Common Prayer*, which has a narrator. Charlotte is the main character, but Grace is the narrator.

BlackBook: Has the written word been devalued since you began your career?

JD: I think specifically novels because people don't understand unreliable narrators, for example; they believe that anything the narrator of a novel tells them is supposed to be the truth. They read a novel as if they were reading nonfiction. They literally do not seem to grasp the difference. And even if they know that one is fiction and one is not, they don't know it at a level where it allows them to not trust a character—they will turn against that character rather than simply think, "This is an interesting, untrustworthy character."

MD: I also think that many people don't make any distinction between an essay and a memoir or confession, and I always want to be really clear with people that for me an essay is an outward inquiry, it's trying to figure out a problem, and I would never ever sit down to write an essay unless it was going to transcend my own experience.

JD: Right, but it is built on personal reference points because an essay has an "I" in it.

MD: Yeah, but it's not memoir. Memoir is allowed to stop at the end of the specific experience, and I think the essay demands transcendence and a thesis. I don't see it as confessional, because I think you should know everything about the narrator but nothing about the author, which I always felt you pulled off beautifully. As readers, we're very much at arm's length the whole time.

JD: Very few people realized that.

BlackBook: So it doesn't ever feel that you are exposing yourselves to other people's scrutiny.

JD: I didn't feel that way, no. As I said, there came a point where so many people thought that I was exposed to their scrutiny that I was unable to respond adequately to the emotional weight that they were laying on it.

MD: Can you remember any specifics?

JD: There was just a lot of mail that I was unable to answer. I couldn't deal with everybody's baggage in a way.

BlackBook: You said in one of your essays collected in *The White Album*, "If I believed that going to a barricade would affect man's fate in the slightest, I would go to that barricade, but it would be less than honest to say that I expect to happen on such a happy ending." You wrote that in 1970. Do you still feel the barricades are ineffective?

JD: I don't think that they are effective, but I think that sometimes you have to go to them, but in full knowledge that it's futile. The huge demonstrations here and in Europe before the Iraq war did not delay the course of that war, and I always thought that with Vietnam it was less the demonstrations than the fact that it was brought home to large numbers of voters that this was a no-win and people were getting killed and money was being spent and it wasn't getting anywhere.

MD: It was all before my time, but I always wondered how much of the antiwar hippie movement was really an aesthetic manifestation.

JD: A lot of that *was* aesthetic.

MD: But would you characterize the counterculture as an upper-middle-class thing?

JD: No, as a middle-class phenomenon. There was a huge new middle class created by World War II and the G.I. bill.

BlackBook: Why do you write?

JD: To figure out what I'm thinking. I really just don't go around most days with a lot of clearly formed thoughts in my head, or even reactions to things. So in order, at least, to stay sentient I have to write.

MD: I find that, too. I don't literally know what I'm thinking until I start writing, but sometimes I feel that once I do arrive at the thing it then feels separate, and it's almost like a conceit, and it doesn't seem authentic in some ways, but you have to go with it.

JD: Which is what's so scary about it.

ALAIN DE BOTTON

People look at you strangely if you make a trip to the zoo without a child. You should ideally have a gang of children, evidence of dribbled Cornetto ice cream cones, and some balloons as well. Contemplating zoo enclosures with oriental small-clawed otters or leopard geckos hardly seems an adult way to pass the afternoon. The elegant question is have you caught the new Tate Mondrians, not the new pygmy hippo at Regent's Park Zoo.

But my five-year-old nephew pulled out at the last minute (he'd remembered it was his best friend's birthday), and I stubbornly decided to go through with our afternoon as planned. My first thought—after buying an ice cream, though not a balloon—was how strange animals look. Apart from the odd cat, horse, or dog, it's been years since I've seen a real animal, an extraordinary *Jungle Book*-ish sort of creature. Take the camel: a U-shaped neck, two furry pyramids, eyelashes that seem coated in mascara, and a set of yellow buck teeth. There was a guide on hand with some facts. Camels can go ten days in the desert without drinking. Their humps aren't filled with water. It's fat. The eyelashes are designed to keep out sand-storms and their liver and kidneys extract all moisture from food, leaving their dung dry and compact. They're some of the best-adapted creatures on the planet, concluded the guide—at which point I experienced a childish burst of jealousy at the inadequacy of the human liver and kidney, and our lack of furry bumps to cut out the need for a mid-afternoon snack.

If creatures end up looking strange, it's a sign of their adaptation to the natural environment, said Darwin, and no one would doubt it in Regent's Park. The Sri Lankan sloth bear has long, mobile lips and two missing upper incisors so that it can suck ants and termites out of their nests, a distinc-tive facial feature which no one who relies on lunch from a deli would bother with. I had some melancholy thought finishing my Cornetto and staring at some tar-colored pygmy hippos wallowing in the mud.

The word *dinosaur* came to mind, not that they resembled them, but they evoked the dinosaur as a byword for fatally slow adaptation to an environment. There are only a few of them left in the world; the future in their natural African habitats lies with lither, more libidinous, gazelle-like things.

A zoo visit proves the cliché that it takes all sorts. Every crea-ture seems woefully adapted for some things, hopelessly suited for others. The horseshoe crab could never get in the pages of *Vogue* (it looks like a miniature Nazi helmet with bowlegs), and couldn't read Gibbon, but it's a star at surviving in deep water and not getting eaten by sharks. It lives quietly, sliding occasionally across the ocean floor to grab a mollusk ("scuttling across the floors of silent seas," for T. S. Elliot fans).

It's hard not to identify with animals, not to land on creatures one might name if forced into an after-dinner round of what-would-you-be-if-you-had-to-be-an-animal game (sadly losing out to Pictionary as evening entertainment). Flaubert loved the game; in his letters, he compared himself variously to a boa constrictor (1841), an oyster in its shell (1845), and a hedgehog rolling up to protect itself (1853). I came away identifying with the Malayan tapir, the baby okapi, the llama, and the turtle (especially on Sunday evenings).

A zoo unsettles, simultaneously making animals more human and humans more animal. "Apes are man's closest relative," reads a caption by the orangutan enclosure, "How many similarities can you see?" Far too many for comfort, of course. Shave him, and dress him in a T-shirt and track suit bottoms, and the one cousin scratching his nose in the corner of the cage is a cousin of mine, except that Jo has a large flat in Belsize Park and spent two weeks in Dorset with his kids this summer. In May 1842, Queen Victoria visited Regent's Park Zoo, and in her diary noted of the orangutan from Calcutta: "he is wonderful, preparing and drinking his tea, but he is painfully and disagreeably human." (Reading this, I imagined being captured and placed in a cage like a room in a Holiday Inn Express, with three meals a day passed through a hatch, and nothing to do other than watch TV—while a crowd of giraffes look at me, giggling and videoing, while commenting on what a short neck I have.)

Inevitably, perhaps, I walk out of the zoo with a pair of Desmond Morris spectacles. Calling Sarah up for dinner loses its innocence; it's merely part of the mating ritual of the human species, not fundamentally different from what llamas are up to when they start to whistle strangely at each other on autumn nights. Then again, there is relief to be found in the ability to view one's antics as complex manifestations of essentially simple animal drives—for food, shelter, and survival of one's genetic offspring. I'll be taking out a yearly zoo membership.

Santa Shrink

AUGUSTEN BURROUGHS

Growing up, I was aware that other families had rituals steeped in more tradition than our own family rituals. There were families that decorated the house for the holidays, raised and lowered the American flag, went on vacation each summer to a lake in upstate New York. There were families that ticked the wall with pencil marks to commemorate every inch.

In my family, the only ritual occurred each fall when my mother suffered a psychotic breakdown and had to be hospitalized. Two weeks before she became completely unglued, I saw the signs in her eyes. They become wide and black and wild, as though she'd become inhabited by something perverted and absolutely ravenous.

Like clockwork, when the colorful leaves began to fall from the trees, my mother began to write one of her massive poems.

Her "breakthrough" works, one of which was sure to deliver her to international literary fame. And in would come the psychiatrist, a man who dressed like Santa Claus year-round. He would put her in the passenger seat of his old Buick and drive her to a distant motel with a small swimming pool and an ice machine, where he would then medicate and "talk" her through the "episode."

Two weeks later, she would be returned in a deflated, empty-sack-like condition. Then I would begin my own ritual of trying to blow her back up again. "It'll be the last time," I promised, endlessly. "You will be famous, you'll see." I told myself that having a mother who went crazy every fall was like having a mother who was a rock star and went on tour.

In my world, birthdays came and went without remark. And Christmas might fall on a Wednesday in June because my mother decided, like the song says, "That we need a little Christmas. Right this very minute."

So as an adult, I had no sense of ritual. Beyond this, I had no sense of anything remotely regular. Which is why I never paid my bills on time. I couldn't even manage to cross the street and hand the garage a check for my Jeep Wrangler's parking space. Thus, the Jeep was claimed by the garage and Chrysler Financial sent their tarantulas after me.

Until I was in my early thirties, I never sent a birthday, Christmas, or anniversary card. Not because I didn't think to, but because I could never get it together in time. I had no training in this simple, respectful task. I specialized in chaos. In nearly destroying myself, and then rebuilding myself, which is exactly what I watched my mother do, year after year, throughout my childhood. It's amazing how this happens. How you become your parents, even though you are determined not to. And sometimes, you become them in ways that are quite transparent to your own eyes. Such as, becoming the opposite.

My brother, for example, never drinks. Okay, I exaggerate. When I was fourteen and he was twenty-one, and we were backstage after the first performance of the Kiss Dynasty world tour, my brother had a Heineken. He was celebrating because he had designed and built all the fire-spitting, rocket-shooting electric guitars himself, in his bedroom, from scratch. But he left half the beer in the bottle. And then, again, when my first memoir hit the *New York Times* bestseller list, my brother had another beer. But that is it. This is because our father was an alcoholic who drank and seemed somewhat homicidal around the edges. In this way, my brother is exactly like my father. Both have a complex relationship with booze. For my brother, as for my father, alcohol isn't something to be sipped at weddings. It is far more than this. It's big, it's powerful. It's a sword over their heads.

I had no trouble slipping into the bottle myself, like an olive.

My mother was going to become a famous writer. But she did not. Instead, I became a writer. In my determination to be nothing like her, I became exactly what she wanted to be. I became my mother. And as a drunk, I became my father. I became a union of the two. Utterly, entirely, their son.

Except, every fall, I do not go crazy. But I write a book. I write it all at once, consumed by the process. Unable to do one thing besides. It has become my ritual.

It is as if a psychiatrist dressed like Santa has come in his Buick and taken me away to a motel. Uncanny, really.

April Foolery

SAM LIPSYTE

Nobody's quite certain when April Fool's Day began, although most scholars point to Pope Gregory XIII's institution of the modestly named Gregorian Calendar in 1582. Many ancient cultures, including the Hindus and the Romans, had celebrated the new year on April 1st, but the new calendar forced humanity to get loaded and wear dumb hats in the middle of winter instead. Some people, however, out of defiance or sheer ignorance, did not acknowledge the switch and this became known as April fools (or fish in France). They were taunted and tricked, and in some countries, pummeled on the buttocks. Though the true meaning of the holiday—to persecute people who may simply be misinformed—has been lost, the prankish spirit endures.

Pranks provide catharsis in any age. We love to see people make fools of themselves because it distracts us from our own idiocies. Even being the prankee has its own blessings: Once we've tripped our tied-together shoelaces or realized that our best friend was using a fake nose, a certain relief courses through us. We are not at the edge of the abyss, after all—we are simply April fools (or fish in France). With that in mind, I offer a half-dozen April Fool's Day pranks guaranteed to lighten the burden of existence.

- Pretend you hit your head and have amnesia. Ask friends, "Who am I? Where's Melanie?" Break into the house of someone you vaguely knew in high school. Draw a bubble bath and wait.

- Call your father and tell him he's gay.

- Send out a press release to Oprah Winfrey apologizing for that stuff you said to your friends about how she's ruining American culture.

- Make a long, deep incision in your torso and sew it up with fishing tackle. Tell people you had your organs stolen. Who's gonna know?

- Visit your grandma. Take money from her purse in front of her. Buy some crack. When the rocks are gone, say "April Fool's, Grandma!"

- Revert to the old Julian calendar. Stand in the middle of Times Square at midnight on March 31. When a policeman tells you to move along, wish New York City's finest a happy New Year and ask him to pummel your buttocks.

Bullets and Brandy and Ice Dust

DBC PIERRE

It's Monday. I'm in a house with an unexploded rocket-propelled grenade embedded in its basement floor. A hole gapes through two stories and a roof. I look out onto white mountains in the backyard and see how comfortably within range we are, not only of rocket-propelled greetings, but also of other, more simple, Kalashnikov-type entertainments.

And I can't help thinking—this is fucking romance.

Granted, I've had some brandy. It's minus twenty-five outside. Minus thirty inside. And I'm not saying romance is the first thing to cross the mind of the man whose house we're in. Still, a hospitable type, he takes me downstairs to see the missile. We approach it as you approach gentle breathing from a darkened crib. It's there, waiting. The shaft sticks a foot out of the floor. When it doesn't wake up, he kicks it.

We remain unexploded.

And when we leave the house for the icy quiet outside, there stand these mountains with a hostile border on them. Right there in the yard. The mighty Caucasus, glorious humps of ice cream with nuts and topping sparkling against a fat blue sky. Close enough to scratch and sniff. And the sky's fat stays blue when the sun falls, like a swimming pool getting deeper, and a moon comes up as bright as sun shimmering under water. And there's this hostile border, sparkling, in front of it, in the near depths.

And I ask—Why, is this romance?

To ponder the question, I retire to a gully between mountains. Here, for no apparent reason, are two old portable cabins, set apart from each other. One is green, and is a kitchen. One is yellow, and has a table. Between them they form a restaurant. It has no name. I sit in the trailer with the table, waiting for the lady with the funky burger apron and the unconvinced face to cross the snow with some barbecued meat. And I ponder this question of romance. I ponder that crucial component of romance that is isolation, being outside of, at odds with, the wider environment: being forced to carve a lonely niche in lieu of wider acceptance by the world. The type of romance that accounts for great music, that recognizes the gusts of misery that lap at our coats trying to suck our warm pretensions. Because weren't the great Russian symphonies just cries from souls acknowledging the unreachability of things? Were they not, in a way, just extravagant sighs?

If this is true, then I've found the romantic ideal, here in the snow, under a nutty cloud of dung smoke, in a place where sounds ring clear, like coins dropped in a cathedral. At the safer end of the Caucasus chain, on Armenia's border with Azerbaijan. Less than a five-hour flight from London. I came because the heroine in my next novel hails from this part of the world. And there's only so much research you can do without sniffing the breeze for yourself.

But high romance on this scale was unexpected. Although somehow I sensed it coming on the plane, I put it down to the romantic traits of flight itself, that type of suspension that happens in the haze of kerosene, perfume, and coffee. Night flight, incidental lighting, gentle murmurs. Screaming frozen tube in the sky. It's a cocoon that sucks a shell off you, opens you out in some way. Feelings are sweeter on airplanes, music sticks harder to the soul. That kind of romance, I guess, is what I'm trying to pinpoint. The kind that comes out to feed after rare, possibly dark situations have smacked your senses awake like veins upraised to a needle. Situations where you're alone with your wits. Places without signposts.

So here's my place. Hayastan, as they call it, was the first firecracker in the Trans-Caucasian string to go bang. It's quiet now, save for an occasional exchange over the Azeri border, whose shadow falls on the quizzical lady carrying barbecued meat. Quiet with its wounds, its smell of dung smoke and gunpowder, poverty and injury. And yet, despite its pain, I find romance not only in its apartness—for much of the border to this landlocked place is closed due to conflict—but in the vivid combustion of spirit that happens in the presence of great opposites. Because within this miasma of chill romance, of searing warm hearts in a forgotten place without resources in the world, there are edges so unspeakably lovely that your spine tingles day and night. The place is painfully beautiful beneath its fractures. A paradise. And I say it without brandy. Hayastan has the warm familiarity of your earliest childhood playroom, your first dog-eared toys strewn in a smell of school-chalk and saliva on skin. An unexpected, unheard-of paradise, where leopards still roam, where forests swish with oak, pistachio, almond, buckthorn, and wild jasmine, where wheat still rustles wild, where apricots and cherries sweeten the air like young sex, where Winston Churchill declared the brandy finer than any cognac, where a lake bigger than Disneyland hides types of trout seen nowhere else on Earth, where the first Christian church arose, where Noah's ark lies trapped on the slopes of a mountain. Where, at minus twenty-five degrees, somebody has hung a towel to dry from the window of an old Soviet apartment, and the towel, so fucking help me, says *Hawaii.*

So another question arises in paradise: To what extent do we *choose* to keep around us the darker, lonelier edges of romance?

When I see the man with the RPG in his basement, I ask him how he can live with such a threat. He says he and his family of six have moved into their tiny garden shed, until the missile is made safe. I ask how long they have been there.

And he says, "Thirteen years. Come, I have some brandy."

My Mother
Was a Monster

RYAN BOUDINOT

I followed my mother's legs through the glistening aisles of Albertson's as she selected items for the Wednesday night meal. We were usually SpaghettiOs-level people, a Hamburger Helper family. We opened our main courses with can openers and dumped the contents into microwave-safe crockery. Our fingernails ripped the glued cardboard seams of boxes that invariably contained "seasoning packets." Most nights my mother dumped upon our table all manner of instant foods, stuff designed to be cooked inside a plastic bag, blobs of starchy substance molten around the edges and frozen solid in the center. To preserve what little domestic dignity she retained, Mom had declared that every Wednesday night we would eat what she called the "fancy meal."

I was the only one among my siblings my mother tolerated as a grocery-shopping partner. It was my responsibility to lobby on my brother and sister's behalf for things we actually wanted to eat. While the nutritional value of our lunches and dinners were always suspect, my parents still held firm to a principle they had established during a brief health-food flirtation in the 1970s—*no sugared cereal.* I steeled myself as we rolled into the cereal aisle, where cartoon characters taunted me from their boxes, pimping the secret prizes within.

I selected a box of Honeycomb, affecting an expression of malnourished need. My mom flattened her wide lips and shook her First Lady hairdo.

"But Mom," I said, "It's *a delicious part of this nutritious breakfast.*"

"Since you and your brother and sister did such a good job cleaning the garage I'll let you splurge and get Frosted Mini-Wheats."

Fuck. Frosted Mini-Wheats hardly counted as sugared cereal. I could hear my sister miming a gag, my brother denouncing it as "fag cereal." I switched tactics and decided to ask for more than I expected, hoping that I could steer my mom to the center, to something like Honey Nut Cheerios. I pulled down a box of Cap'n Crunch.

"Not in a million years. You'll rot your face out. It's either Frosted Mini-Wheats or you're getting Grape-Nuts."

"Crispy Wheats 'n Raisins?"

"*Patrick.*"

"Okay. Frosted Mini-Wheats."

We lived in the kind of neighborhood every American should be familiar with by now. Kids throwing newspapers from bikes?

Check. Shirtless man with hairy nipples on front porch waving to the mailman? Check. Teenage dude blasting Judas Priest from his GTO? Misogynistic signage on a treehouse? Lady with a big butt gardening in mismatching yellow plaids? Check, check, check.

My brother and sister, Greg and Yvonne, bore down on the station wagon to paw through the groceries as soon as we pulled into the driveway. Yvonne quickly located her feminine items and hid them inside her sweatshirt. Greg scrutinized his canister of muscle-bulking powder upon which an oiled wall of musculature flexed. Here's everything you need to know about my siblings: they were both in high school, had both had sex with their respective partners in our basement rec room (when the rest of us weren't home) and had both told me about these experiences in graphic detail.

"Quit digging through the bags, just get everything inside!" my mom said. My mom's name was Lorraine, and she looked like a Lorraine. Sometimes you see people who look so much like their names it's as though their features conformed to whatever their parents decided to call them. On the other hand, I felt I had been poorly named. For years I had been trying to convince my parents to let me legally change my name from Patrick to Lars. Watching a show on transexuals one night, I suddenly understood: I was a Lars trapped in the name of a Patrick.

Greg was openly breaking one of the rules of the household—no heavy metal on the living room stereo. My mom hissed at him to turn it off, which struck me as ironic; the song presently vibrating the Hummel figurines perched on the speakers was about authority figures who don't appreciate the need to party on overdrive. With the plastic bags sagging on the kitchen island, Greg quickly located the offensive box of cereal and squinted cruelly at me. "Hey, Patrick, check it out. Did you know that Frosted Mini-Wheats are really popular in San Francisco? Know what I mean? *San* Fran*cisco*?"

We proceeded to slap-fight. Greg put me in a headlock and hissed into my ear, "Your choice. My armpit or my fart? I'm giving you three seconds to decide which one to smell. Armpit or fart?"

"Greg, just put away the darn groceries. Patrick, go check on the main course."

I wiggled out of my brother's grip, got in one good slap, then trudged down to the basement and opened the freezer. I had left it propped open with a can of tuna so Carl could get some air, and had given him one of my windbreakers so he wouldn't get too cold. Still, I found the kid shivering and sniffling, sitting on bags of frozen peas and carrots, eating a freezer-burned Halloween cookie in the shape of a witch hat. Carl was in my grade and played goalie on my soccer team, a position he had attained through sheer nepotism, being that his dad was the coach.

"W-what are you d-doing?" Carl said.

"Shut up, Carl. Now listen, okay? I happen to know my mom wants to make you for dinner, but we're all hoping for pizza pockets instead. She makes crummy stews."

Carl started crying again and I had to put my hand over his mouth to ensure his pleas for mercy couldn't be heard up through the laundry chute. A toilet flushed upstairs; my dad was home. The walls of the basement reverberated with the ambient noise of moving sewage.

"When you hear the toilet flush two times, that's your signal that it's okay to escape. Just go up the stairs and turn left, go out the back porch and make sure the door doesn't slam shut. You're going to have to wade across the creek to the woods, then head toward the high school. You should be safe by the time you reach it. And run fast. My mom did track and field in college."

Carl nodded. I returned upstairs, my stomach growling as I imagined the gooey interior of a combo-flavored pizza pocket.

My dad, guy by the name of Dean, worked at a local factory that made crayons, doing something he called "Planning Guidelines." At barbecuelike events he would brag that he had "put pressure on top management" to change the name of the "flesh" crayon. All we knew was that when they fucked up a color, we got the rejects. Today there had been a mistake with a batch of red-orange; it had come out too much like orange-red. Several misshapen bricks of this color sat on the dining room table.

My father and I performed our eight-part secret handshake. "Patrick, buddy. What the H-E-double-toothpicks did you learn in school today?"

"Photosynthesis," I said.

"Hey, that's cool. Well if you need to use my camera, just lemme know." My dad swept my mother up in his arms and twirled her around the kitchen. "Lorraine, my dear! Let's forget about inept pigment technicians who can't tell the difference between Yellow No. 8 and Orange No. 3, okay? I'm starving. What's for dinner?"

"His name is Carl," my mom said.

I fell to the kitchen linoleum clutching my side and cried out.

"Patrick, what happened? What is it?" my mother said.

"Oh my God . . . appendix . . . rupturing . . . the pain. . . ."

My mom palpated my abdomen then helped me to the upstairs bathroom. I kind of pretended to fall against the toilet and accidentally flush it. Groaning, I flailed my arms around and pretended to accidentally flush it again. My mom stood over me with her hands on her hips. I imagined Carl climbing out of the freezer with Halloween-colored cookie sprinkles on his lips, shivering in my windbreaker, ascending the stairs. I heard the back screen door slam shut. An expression of panic must have passed over me. My mom scowled and said, "Hey, what's going on here?"

Yvonne screeched from her room and raced to join us. "Oh my God, Mom, I totally saw Carl running across our yard."

My mother growled at me. "There's be consequences," she said, then fetched one of her axes from behind the toilet bowl. "Well are you just going to sit there stupidly, or are you going to help me get that little snot-nosed jerk?"

Dusk had begun to overtake our backyard, but I was able to see Carl escaping through the trees on the other side of the creek. I should have lent him my cammo jacket. Holding the axe aloft, my mother led us on a chase for our supper. I managed to keep up for the most part, while my brother surged ahead and my dad and sister lagged behind. I knew Carl wasn't swift on his feet; there was a reason our team was in last place in our division. I just hoped he could make it to the high school. While I dreaded the prospect of a dinner of Carl, I found myself sort of admiring my mother as she leapt over fallen trees and hacked her way through sticker bushes in pursuit of her quarry. I certainly couldn't imagine David Thompson's or Nick Peterson's moms wielding an axe at full speed through the woods without getting a single snag in their panty hose. My brother, showing off his tight-end skills, tackled Carl and pinned him to the forest floor. Soon we were standing in a semicircle, breathing hard, staring into the terrified eyes of the worst goalie I had ever known. My mother raised her axe. The muscles in her neck tightened and her eyes went unnaturally wide as she bellowed a war cry. The noise should have been recorded and used as a sound effect for a movie about a bunch of people who attack each other and stuff. Yes indeed, birds rose from trees into the sky upon hearing it, signifying impending terror.

My dad loudly cleared his throat. "Now Lorraine, let's just think this through a little bit here."

My mother's death-blow wail pathetically trailed off, like a safe and sane sparkling cone firework. My dad gently pried the axe from her hands and put his arm around her shoulder. I knew then that a man with guts enough to call a crayon "racist" was a man who could dissuade my mother from cannibalism.

"We love your cooking, honey, it's just . . . we're kind of tired of fancy night."

"Is it how I prepare them? I can try a different recipe."

Greg helped Carl to his feet. "You don't have to impress us with your cooking, Mom," he said.

"We like the instant stuff better," I said.

"So are you like going to kill him or what?" my sister said.

I sneered back at her. "Are you crazy? Why kill someone for dinner when there's pizza pockets and mini drumstick bites at home?"

"Hey, here's an idea," my dad said, "Let's let Carl go so he can continue his goalie duties on Patrick's team."

"Yeah, let him go so they can suck another day," Greg said, frowning at me, pointing to his armpit, his ass, his nose.

Carl sprinted, crying, through the woods toward the high school. My mother called plaintively after him, "Carl, honey, be sure to tell your mother I have something I want to donate to the YWCA raffle."

As we walked home, I could tell my sister was a little disappointed we weren't having fancy night. My brother and dad reenacted football plays from mythic games, leaping over exposed roots and mossy stumps with pretend footballs tucked under their arms. I asked my mother if I could carry the axe. Sounding worn out, she said sure and handed it to me. I took a couple swings at some randomly selected trees and ran my finger down the worn handle, where she had cut a number of notches with a pocket knife, each notch representing a fancy night.

I had assumed we would have pizza pockets in lieu of Carl for dinner that night, but I had assumed wrong. My mother still held me accountable for the meal that got away, and as punishment assigned me the purposeless task of sweeping the basement. I pushed the broom back and forth across the concrete, my stomach growling forlornly. All the embarrassing phases my family had undergone were on display down here, a graveyard of exercise machines, a karaoke unit with a microphone repaired with layers of duct tape. The worn-out couch, where my brother and sister had laid their respective mates. The ancient TV with the enigmatic UHF dial and an antenna you had to wiggle to catch a signal. A floor-to-ceiling stack of cartons of discontinued, Caucasian-resembling crayons. I listened to my family chatter and laugh upstairs and fantasized that they had forgotten I even existed. I would live down here while they went about the business of eating healthy cereal and watching nature documentaries on TV. I could live down here for years, sleep on the couch, subsist on frozen cookie dough, draw some beige things, get a lot of exercise.

My mother opened the door to the basement, interrupting my train of thought. "Patrick, when you're done sweeping, could you pick out some leftovers to bring up?"

I said sure, and leaned the broom against the wall. The freezer was still open from Carl's escape. I peered inside at all the foil-wrapped packages, the ones labeled with names of kids I used to know, wondering what sounded good for dinner.

The Hemingway Challenge

Ernest Hemingway was once challenged to write a story in six words. The result: "For sale, baby shoes, never used." It's rumored that Hemingway thought it his greatest work, and it's invariably offered as the model for what micro-fiction should aspire to. Stirred by this great masterpiece, we asked twenty-five of today's literary lights to offer their own original six-word story.

"Forgive me!" "What for?" "Never mind."

—JOHN UPDIKE

Eyeballed me, killed him. Slight exaggeration.

—IRVINE WELSH

Satan—Jehovah—fifteen rounds. A draw.

—NORMAN MAILER

Saigon hotel. Decades later. He weeps.

—ROBERT OLEN BUTLER

My nemesis is dead. Now what?

—MICHAEL CUNNINGHAM

Father died. Mother triumphed. I left.

—MARY GAITSKILL

Oh, that? It's nothing. Not contagious.

—AUGUSTEN BURROUGHS

As she fell, her mind wandered.

—REBECCA MILLER

It's negative. Say hi to Mom.

—BEN GREENMAN

All her life: half a house.

—JAMIE O'NEILL

Grass, cow, calf, milk, cheese, France.

—RICK MOODY

She gave. He took. He forgot.

—TOBIAS WOLFF

He remembered something that never happened.

—AM HOMES

Tossed remorselessly, whiffle balls sure hurt.

—JT LeRoy

Havana's no place for hockey, coach.

—Nicholas Weinstock

I saw. I conquered. Couldn't come.

—David Lodge

Mother's Day came, doubling Oedipus' pleasure.

—Bruce Benderson

Poison; meditation; skiing; ants—nothing worked.

—Edward Albee

"Cyanide? Bitter almonds." He knew. How?

—Brian Bouldrey

"You? Her? No dice, fact boy."

—Pinckney Benedict

Shiva destroys Earth: "Well, that's that."

—AG Pasquella

You are not shit. You are!

—A Memoir: Jerry Stahl

"Welcome to Moeshe Christiansen's bar mitzvah."

—Andrea Seigel

24-Hour Party People: Irvine Welsh Meets Damien Hirst

Despite us being bracketed together as big carousing buddies by numerous newspapers, I'd never actually met Damien Hirst. We've managed to acquire a lot of common acquaintances, even some mutual friends, over the last few years. Bizarrely, we've even been mistaken for each other on occasion: each having had to account for the other's conduct. So it probably was time that we actually met.

A good time as it happens; both Damien and I have cleaned up our acts in recent years, meaning that a head-to-head would be semi-coherent and that an intermediary wasn't essential. *BlackBook* provided journalist Craig McLean to help put things on track when we rambled, but basically left us to get on with it.

My knowledge of the art world is far from comprehensive, but I know that Damien Hirst's ascendancy within it has been meteoric. While still a student at Goldsmiths College he curated the widely acclaimed Freeze exhibition. This brought his work into contact with the art dealer Charles Saatchi. After graduating he presented *In and Out of Love*, an installation for which he filled a gallery with hundreds of live tropical butterflies, some spawned from monochrome canvases on the wall. With *The Physical Impossibility of Death in the Mind of Someone Living* (1991), his infamous tiger shark in a glass tank of formaldehyde shown at the Saatchi Gallery, Damien Hirst became a media icon and household name. He has since been imitated, parodied, reproached, and exalted by the media and public alike. Having won the Turner Prize in 1995, and redefined how we see dead farmyard animals, he has become the contemporary artist most referenced by the media, and the standard-bearer of Brit Art.

While revered, Hirst has inevitably had his critics. Irritating crusty right-wingers and gathering shock headlines from the tabloids may not be any artist's raison d'être, but it's an amusing diversion and definitely does one no harm. Probably more important are the criticisms that come from within the art world. The Stuckist Movement, which exists to advance the cause of painting as "the most vital artistic means of addressing contemporary issues," claims that his work is boring and unremarkable. Substantially, though, their criticisms amount to more of a critique of modern conceptual art in general rather than of Damien Hirst himself. "In the nineteenth century, the art establishment was sure of its greatness. Critics, artists, collectors, and curators agreed that the standards they proclaimed were of great art and would endure. They were wrong. The current art establishment is likewise sure of its greatness. They are also wrong."

How long the tears will flow for the so-called masterpieces of British modern art destroyed in May in Charles Saatchi's East London warehouse fire is debatable. However, only time will tell whether conceptual art is a fad, or whether it's a painting, as a medium, that now cannot adequately portray the complexity of modern life.

I meet Damien Hirst at his West End offices, named Science. His bar is called Pharmacy: There's always been something of the mad scientist about his public persona. In the flesh, though, he is relaxed, warm, and grounded, still speaking in a not-overdone working-class Leeds accent.

It was an opportune time to meet in more ways than one. The previous day I had just heard about the Saatchi warehouse fire. It seemed as good a place to start as any, once we'd cleared up a few mistaken identity details.

Irvine Welsh: We've never actually met before, but we've always been attributed as hanging out together.

Damien Hirst: Once in a bar I ended up starting a fight with somebody, and as we broke it off they went, "Fuck off Irvine." I'd just shaved my head and I think they thought I was you, so I got you a very bad reputation. There was probably one night when you were starting a fight simultaneously up north and in London. Or maybe they thought I was Eddie Irvine [an Irish racing driver]. There was that great quote in the paper when he was being linked with Claudia Schiffer, and somebody went up to him and said, "Is it true that you're having an affair with Claudia Schiffer?" and he went, "I wouldn't touch that fat cunt with a barge pole."

IW [*Laughing*]: That's fucking fantastic . . . I don't know enough about the contemporary art world to make judgments about it, but I was interested in that fire and what's been written about it.

DH: We thought maybe [Charles] Saatchi had done it. He buys in bulk, right across the board. You get sick of it—have a clean out.

IW: When I write a book, the manuscript is actually worthless once it's gone into the process, but in your case you have an artefact, and the artefact can be destroyed. How does that feel?

DH: Well, with technology today things can be remade, so there's a dilemma as to what is the most important thing—what the artist was trying to communicate at the time, or the actual object itself? I've lost about seventeen paintings now, the spin paintings, and I can make another spin painting, but it would never be the same as the ones I've lost.

IW: But would you want to remake them, or would you think, "Oh, I've fucking left that behind, there's no interest there."

DH: Well there's one piece I lost that is called *I Want to Spend the Rest of My Life Everywhere with Everyone*—it's two bits of glass together with a paint-sprayer and a Ping-Pong ball on it. I'm finding out about whether I can get the old paint-sprayer because if I can't get the old paint-sprayer then I can't really remake it, because it's not going to look like the same thing, it's not going to work in the same way, but I think if it's a fire, you have to say, "Well they're gone." Because that's what fire does. And you could end up spending your whole life trying to make your old stuff.

IW: The only thing I can compare it to is sometimes I have been banging away, you know, and get into this transcendental stage where you're usually doing your best stuff, and let's just say that you're tired and you make mistakes and you don't back up your discs, and you hit the fucking wrong key and you've just lost a few chapters, and you think, "I can't fucking take this," and I've taken the computer and thrown it across the room. I've just sat down and cried or I've even tried to retype it as quickly as possible, but even if you replicate it better, you never actually believe that you have. You feel that it's outside that moment and it's never going to be the same. You just feel a little bit of the magic has gone.

DH: The worst thing is if I lose titles, because you can be hammered out of your mind and you just fucking forget the title of something you've been trying to work out for a year, and the next day you just can't remember it—you're fucked.

IW: Usually with books it's the title that comes first with me.

DH: Same with me. I've got titles that I'm working on that I haven't even got the sculpture for. I've got one called *Devoured by a Desire to Walk in Front of You with a Duvet Until You Die.* But that just came as a title. Fuck knows what it will look like, but something to do with having kids.

But in a way it's quite reassuring that things can die, do you know what I mean? Somewhere between the unique objects and the mass-produced objects, between the Coke can and the *Mona Lisa*, it's nice to live in a world where you do have both those options all the time. But sometimes you need to take them away to appreciate them, unfortunately.

BlackBook: Would you want someone to read an early draft of one of your novels, or someone to see an early version of one of your sculptures?

DH: No, someone once came into my studio when I had builders and diggers and fucking machines, and they said, "You must love all this," and I said, "I fucking hate it," and they said, "What's your favorite bit?" and I said, "When it's all fucked off and there's just the art work." People think you must really love all the process.

IW: With books you just want to type "The End" and send it off to the editor; you just want to get to that point. There's a creative side that you actually enjoy, but then after that it's just a fucking slog to get the thing looking reasonably okay, you know.

I was interested in one of the things you once said—that you want people to react to art the way they react to medicine.

DH: Well I think art gets boring pretty fast and to give it relevance today is pretty difficult; you've got to catch people out visually, so I think you're always looking for that, and I thought that pills were a brilliant little form, better than any minimalist artist. They're all designed to make you buy them.

IW: This is the thing, there's a design concept for everything, whereas before it was just really functional.

DH: I mean pills do come out of flowers, plants, things from the ground, and it makes you feel good, you know, to just have a pill to feel beauty.

BlackBook: That's why when Es came out people took such care to design them, putting Mitsubishi logos and stuff on them.

DH: Brilliant.

IW: Yeah, they were great. You just fucking couldn't beat them. I've stopped taking them now, but I aim to actually start again in a couple of years' time.

DH: Yeah, I've thought about it actually; I've got loads of mates and they're still doing the charlie [coke], and you just go, "You're fucking mad, it's better to have the Es; at least you have a laugh—you're fucking miserable on charlie."

IW: I used to enjoy the hangovers and come-downs to write, that was always a good time for me, but what I've found just over the last five years is that's changed a lot. I used to feel this nastiness and strangeness, and I used to really want to attack that feeling, and fight through it, almost, on the keyboard, but now I just want to lie in bed and feel sorry for myself. That's the only reason I've stopped.

DH: I think it's a young man's game; it's really attractive on youngsters, but when you get older you just look like a miserable cunt.

IW: I've taken up long-distance running and boxing and all this kind of stuff, so I'm getting the buzz from endorphins now, you know. It's partly the old fucking vain stupid reason like going out with a younger bird, but I think the other reason is that I really do get the endorphin buzz through exercise.

DH: How old are you?

IW: Forty-five. And I've taken up boxing as well—coldly going into a boxing ring and getting hit is a weird, weird thing but you realize that it's not actually that painful; it's more of an annoyance than pain. You realize that your mentality changes, and you see it for what it is. It's an exploratory thing for me, and it's as interesting doing this now as taking drugs was ten, twenty years ago for me.

DH: I think creatively, any great writers or great artists, your whole work is a map of a man's life and it goes through that young to old to slowing-down process, and it's interesting all the way through, and it's very easy to pretend you're young and deny it, as a lot of people do. I think it's much better to get beaten up in a boxing ring than take E.

IW: I want something new to come along that's going to blow me away the same way that Ecstasy did.

BlackBook: Mushrooms, that's the big thing now.

DH: I can't eat them now either.

IW: I can't take acid now—that's really a young man's drug, I think as soon as you become aware of your mortality in your late twenties you just leave that fucking stuff alone, it's too much of a tax on the brain, but mushrooms, because you're not up there for eight hours, but an hour or two at the most, I can just about do. I haven't for a while, but if the opportunity arose and it was a nice hot day. . . .

DH: I stopped drinking when Joe [Strummer] died; he was a really good mate, so we hung out a lot. But he was a fucking nightmare because I was trying to stop drinking for about a year, and Joe was just, fucking, "Have a drink," and I couldn't deal with it, so I always accepted drinks off Joe. So when he died I was just about to have a drink and I thought, "No, fuck it, I won't." And then after that you look around and the quality of the drinkers had really gone down, and the babble and the fucking shit going on, and once you see that you just think, "Fuck off."

IW: I used to love getting fucked up and maybe going into this coma and not even sleeping, just going through to the next day, that was always a great time.

DH: Yeah, me too, I used to love that. Once you get to ten the next morning . . .

IW: . . . you're back in business.

DH: Fucking nightmare, on the phone trying to get more gear [drugs].

IW: But that's the time now that I just listen to all this fucking shite, and think, "I'm not vibing on this."

DH: You go from being the worst to total intolerance.

IW: You do, it's the convert syndrome.

DH: The best thing for me was having kids, and wanting to be at the same state they're in in the morning, but by the time you get used to it they'll be out on fucking drugs and, you know—I suppose I'll start again when they're eighteen.

IW: I always drank heavily, it's been a cultural thing, but I think a lot of what sustained it for me has been doing the writing, because you'll be sitting there, typing away, about these people that don't exist—it's a psycho thing to do, really—and when you finish that you just want to go out and celebrate, you want to get fucked for days and months, and you don't want to go back to it again, so you'll do anything not to go back to it.

DH: I definitely had two years in London where I fucking enjoyed and loved every day, and then I probably had a year when I wasn't sure and then another two years when I didn't even admit I wasn't enjoying it. But for two years we were celebrating *every* day.

IW: It's difficult to get to that point of admitting to yourself when it stops becoming a validation of life, and starts becoming an escape, or a way of avoiding getting on with something else. I think you do have to tear the arse out off it and make a complete cunt of yourself before you get to that point.

I watched this thing on Channel 5, this ultimate reality TV documentary thing, *Bumfight*.

DH: Oh yeah, my brother told me about it yesterday, he said it was fucking evil. How can you show it on TV?

IW: I just wondered what you thought about this whole reality TV thing. I was over in the States and they were telling me that the reality TV bubble has burst, but coming back here it's obviously as strong as ever.

DH: In a way it's like real life, it exhausts you and you need to go out and see a movie to get it all out of your head. All that *Jackass* stuff, though, I fucking love all that.

BlackBook: Has Pop Idol had a positive impact on pop culture?

IW: I don't know, I'm in two minds about it. Music is a commodity, so why not accept that and produce your pop stars that way and get rid of them that way. There's always going to be a place for disposable pop stars because that's what kids want, basically. It's probably as good a way as any of selecting them.

DH: I think the big thing that fucks it up is that no matter how good the talent is it all happens so fucking fast in the media, you get this big bubble and then they begin to believe this bullshit and start to rely on it, and then it gets taken away and you're fucked.

IW: I think there's something about having a reason to celebrate. People now support big soccer clubs like Manchester United, so they can celebrate something, basically, and you think to yourself, "What are they actually doing to merit this celebration?" and I think this is part of the culture as well—that everything is an event to celebrate. I'm about to sign a contract to do a book, so I've got a reason to celebrate, but this is a culture that just wants to fucking celebrate for its own sake.

DH: The worst thing is that people come to your studio when you're working on stuff, and go, "That's brilliant, that's fucking brilliant," just to get their hand in, and you know it's shit, so you end up in this situation where the only person you can trust is yourself.

IW: I can't read book critics, for example, it doesn't matter whether it's praise or condemnation. You've got your own shit going on in your head, and to actually engage in somebody else's views. . . .

DH: As Andy Warhol said, you don't read your reviews, you weigh them. I look at sales [rather than reviews]. At least sales admits its own cynicism. I've got some shit reviews recently, and people say, "You must be really upset about that," and I don't actually give a fuck.

IW: I think success does isolate you from that. If somebody is making a shitload of cash they're not really going to bother about bad reviews, but for somebody starting out with their first book or first exhibition a review is everything.

DH: I've always tried to ignore the money and focus on the art. You get massive responsibility with money, and that's something I found very difficult, and then you get scared of the money. Twenty grand I didn't care; a hundred grand I didn't care. But when it started going higher than that suddenly all your mates have changed, and you got mates who aren't your mates. I remember going out for dinner with my mum and a couple of guys, and I was so pissed [drunk] that my dinner went all over the floor in a posh restaurant, and my mum went, "I could pay my gas bill with that money." I went, "I'll pay your gas bill," and she went, "Don't fucking try and buy me." I've always believed that art's more powerful and important than money, but it gets fucking close sometimes, and you just have to stay open to the fact that if you decide money's more important you have to stop doing it.

IW: Money isn't really a reason to do anything; it's a reason not to do things, but it's never a reason to do something.

DH: People always say to me, "God you could just sign dog shit and sell it," and you go, "Yeah, I could, but why the fuck would I?"

IW: There's that debate now about whether painting is dead or not, or whether modern life, modern society, is so complex, so dynamic that you can't actually capture it on canvas.

DH: I think art's more popular now than it ever was. I don't think I created that, but I definitely cashed in on that. It's probably the most valuable currency in the world, and painting is the best level of art. I always say that if you leave a painting out on the street and it's still there in the morning, it's shit. There are art stores you can go in, and if it was all in a Dumpster you wouldn't nick [steal] anything. I do think painting's been mother-fucked by photography and images and stuff like that, but now that images have been air-brushed people have gone back to painting. It's the only kind of imagery that makes any attempt at honesty.

POSTSCRIPT

Later on in the pub, Craig, a former deputy editor of the *Face* magazine, reminds me of the time when the magazine asked several celebrities to draw something on a Post-it note and send it back to them. I quickly scrawled a penis and pair of bollocks. So too did Damien Hirst. The difference was that somebody in the *Face* wanted to hold on to Damien's offerings—resulting in a letter from his lawyers—while mine, like the rest, probably ended up in the bucket. It must be a strange pressure to have your idle doodlings cast as an original work of art with a value.

Damien doesn't seem like a man under pressure, though, or if he is he's managed to cultivate a good line in nonchalant grace. I enjoyed meeting him; I know this because I now find it hard to use his surname. Whether he'll go down in history as one of the greatest artists of all time, or simply as part of a diversionary footnote called modern conceptual art, is something I haven't got the breadth of knowledge to speculate on. But I do get a hunch—with him at any rate—it'll be the former rather than the latter. Despite a relaxed and engaging manner he maintains that driven bearing of someone whose best work is ahead of him.

It was 1988 and I was nineteen. It was a very hot day, as it often is on Christmas day in Australia, and I spent the day in my mother's house. I had left home, and this house, two years earlier; the day I moved in with one of my high school teachers and vowed never to return.

But I was lonely and friendless in 1988 and had nowhere else to go.

I arrived by taxi. My mother stood on the doorstep waving her hand back and forth, a fast and constant waving, as though frantic to get somebody's attention, somebody far away who might not realize she was there.

When I reached the stoop, she grabbed hold of me and held me tight.

"Helloooo. Hellooooo," she cried.

And I did what I always do when she hugs me this way: I stiffened and returned none of her desperate love.

I walked into the sweltering house: a house in which everything was chipped or broken: half-done D.I.Y. jobs gone bad, gaping holes in the linoleum and net curtains stained orange-brown from my stepfather's chain smoking.

In the corner of the living room stood the two-foot plastic Christmas tree, the same one that came out of its box every year. The tin-foil decorations had already shed their tinsel over the brown couch, brown carpet, brown chairs, and brown cushions.

The little white dog that my stepfather hated whimpered and whined in the back garden; not allowed inside.

I hated myself when I was in that house; for the way I became, for my cruelty, for my obvious and snobbish contempt, and because I did little to hide from my mother the fact that I didn't want to be at home.

For my mother, Christmas day represented the best of the world; its redemptive or "let's start all over again" possibilities.

I sat down at the table.

It was a small gathering: my mother, stepfather, two of my stepfather's golfing friends, and me.

I watched my mother's face, the strain of its forced happiness, the overtired birdlike chirping, "Isn't this great? Aren't we having a wonderful time!"

The more she insisted that we were happy, the more I refused to agree.

"Is everything okay?" she asked me.

I nodded and looked at the chipped plates, chipped glasses (all of them different), and the cheap Christmas crackers.

It wasn't my mother's fault that she was poor, but I was in a foul and snobby state of mind, on a ruthless path to exchanging one kind of life for another.

THE PEOPLE MISSING FROM CHRISTMAS DAY

My brother was in prison that Christmas for a crime the name of which my mother can only whisper, and my father (her ex-husband) was in a psychiatric hospital or prison (or just recently released from one or the other).

We were a few feet away from the room in which my brother had tried to hang himself and the bedroom where my stepfather kept his shotguns, ready for the return of my father.

"Let's open the presents!" my mother chirped.

"After the food," said my stepfather.

And so we waited.

He was boss. She did what he said, always.

She needed me to be on her side, but instead of helping her to feel happy, I used words I knew she didn't have a hope of understanding.

I was going to be studying law in the new year and I wanted her to know how smart I was, how different. But she didn't care how smart I was (I spent six years at University and at the end she didn't know what degrees I had): She only cared that I loved her, loved being near her; that she could make me happy.

THE PHOTOGRAPHS

In a photograph of this Christmas day, we are sitting around the table (which is a pool table covered with a piece of chipboard) and I am wearing a purple paper hat.

There's a plastic rat dangling from my mouth. I must have got the rat out of a Christmas cracker and I have its tail between my teeth.

I'm smiling a convincing smile. Most people who look at this photograph would say I look happy. I have always looked happy in photographs; I have one of those easy, camera-ready smiles, but I know better than most how often photographs lie.

My stepfather is sitting at the head of the table. He's wearing a blue T-shirt, the same kind of grubby blue T-shirt he wears nearly every day. I have never seen him dressed up, with the exception of the day he married my mother in 1983, when he wore a blue suit.

His tattooed arms are folded across his chest, resting on his pot belly, and his blue T-shirt covers his stomach scars and bullet wounds, wounds like craters, the skin around them collapsed like sand caving into a hole.

When you ask my stepfather how he got wounded, he says he was shot when he was out killing kangaroos, in the days when he worked as a forklift driver on the wharves.

I've never believed this story, but I wouldn't tell him that.

My stepfather's friend (I'll call him Peter) looks sad and red in the photograph. He looks red, not because it's a hot day and there is no air-conditioning in the house, but because from the top of his balding scalp all the way down to the ends of his fingers, Peter is covered in red sores and scabs.

Peter's wife (I'll call her Wendy) has black hair in a beehive, and like her husband, looks sad. Wendy has an obsessive-compulsive disorder so chronic that she washes her hands until they bleed and puts Peter's clothes through the washing machine five or six times before considering them clean.

Peter's skin condition explains why there's so much food left on my plate. I couldn't eat.

Perhaps if he hadn't been sitting next to me, his scabby arms hadn't been resting on the table so close to my plate of peas and turkey and gravy, I might have eaten more.

I remember wondering that day whether Wendy's uncontrollable urge to clean has something to do with Peter's skin condition; the sight of pestilent sores that make you feel dirty just from being in the same room as them.

My mother isn't in this photograph, so she must be the one who took it. But there's another photo of her, and like me, she's wearing a purple paper hat and smiling a big smile.

My ability to smile no matter how bad things are is hereditary; what I haven't inherited is my mother's knack for not only smiling through crises, but ignoring critical situations altogether until they become almost life threatening. A kind of unstoppable happy-faced optimism, that although dangerous, I could sometimes use a little more of.

After Christmas lunch, we opened our presents.

I had forgotten to get anything for Peter or Wendy and felt lousy about it, but my mother had put my name on the gift card and they both thanked me for their calendars and kissed me on the cheek.

I wondered what my mother would think of her present. She didn't read much, but she might like this: a cheerful novel by Maeve Binchy, a popular, nonthreatening Irish writer.

She did like it, and I enjoyed her smile when she read the inscription. I could do that: I could write loving inscriptions.

And then I opened my present: a soft-toy polar bear and a piece of jewelry I would never wear.

Later, we moved out to the backyard and I sat in the only patch of shade. It was hot and getting hotter. The blow-flies were landing on our sweating faces and arms and the sound of people in their yards, laughing and talking, seemed to me a kind of torture.

My stepfather and Peter had a few beers and my mother, who never drinks alcohol, talked to Wendy, who is also a teetotaler, about golf.

I pretended to read the newspaper.

"Pull my finger," said my stepfather as he got out of his chair and came toward me.

"No," I said.

"Go on! Pull my finger."

"No!" I said. "I don't want to."

"Go on. Pull my bloody finger!"

It was the same trick every time I saw him.

He'd hound me to pull his finger, and when I did, he farted. A terrible, loud, fart.

"Ha, ha, ha," he laughed, and Peter, who rarely laughed, laughed too.

"Gotcha!"

"You didn't get me," I said, blushing furiously.

The hours passed slowly.

Around six o'clock we ate leftover turkey and ham in sandwiches for tea and then went back into the living room to watch TV:

probably *It's a Wonderful Life* or another film set in a place where Christmas happens in colder, snowy climates.

I wanted to change the channel to something less festive, maybe the news.

"Where's the remote control?" I asked.

"Is my face red?" asked my stepfather.

"Just tell me where it is."

"Is my face red?" he asked again, grinning.

"No," I said, "it isn't red."

"Well it's not up my arse-hole then is it?" he said.

"Ha ha!" he laughed, and so did Peter and Wendy and my mother.

"I better go home," I said. "I have to get to a party."

"Oh no," said my mother. "Aren't you going to stay the night?"

"No," I said, "I promised all my friends I'd come to their party. It's going to be great."

While I waited for the taxi that took more than an hour to come, I was as sad as I can ever remember being.

POSTSCRIPT

Since 1988, I've been back to my mother's house no more than six times, and never at Christmas.

I've spent every Christmas day anywhere but home: with friends and their parents, with boyfriends' families, under the bed, or hiding in a hotel room pretending to be overseas.

Until recently, I lied to my mother every year about my whereabouts on Christmas day.

"Where are you spending Christmas?" my mother would ask,

and every year I'd see the desperate hope in those eyes that get smaller and smaller with age.

"I'm going away to Tasmania with friends," or "I have to go to so-and-so's family's house," or "I have to work."

I thought she knew I was lying all along, but she told me recently that she really had no idea.

"Well, I suppose there's some very bad memories in that house," she said.

My mother is planning to move soon and she may think that will change things: that in the new house I'll come for Christmas.

I should tell her that I'm sorry, and that I'll probably always hate Christmas day, no matter where I am, or what house it's in.

I should tell her I'm sorry and that it's not personal, that it never really was, that Christmas in Australia just can't compete with the Christmases of my childhood in Ireland: the snow (or prospect of snow), the open fire full blazing while presents were opened under a real tree that was sold by a man going from door to door in the days before my brother became a criminal and my father went mad.

Sneakers Make the Boy

JONATHAN AMES

As a young boy I had a shoe fetish. Not to brag, but I was clearly something of a prodigy when it comes to perversion, and my shoe fetish, like most perversions, had a ritualistic aspect, because the whole thing with perversion is build-up, creating a mounting order for the revelation of forbidden delights. Think of the man (a panty-fetishist) who steals panties from female acquaintances:

Step 1: He seizes an opportunity at a dinner party, let's say, to gain access into the acquaintance's bedroom. Then he opens bureau drawers and his heart is pounding deliciously with adrenaline.

Step 2: He finds the panty drawer—bliss. He hesitates—the glory of the moment, all those panties!—and then his hand shoots into the drawer.

Step 3: He grabs a pair of panties, hides them on his person. He then sneaks out of the bedroom and is narcoticized for the rest of the evening, somehow making polite conversation.

Steps 4 and 5: When he gets home, he delays gratification— he clears dishes from the sink, makes phone calls, washes up. Then he gets into bed and examines the panties thoroughly and either puts them on or just stares at them, and in both cases, he manipulates himself to orgasm. Of course what follows is terrible despair and acid self-loathing and promises to himself that this is the last time!

Well, my shoe thing as a boy wasn't as bad as the panty-fetishist described above, but for me getting a new pair of sneakers—my shoe fetish was, to be precise, more of a sneaker fetish—was so stimulating, so exciting, that I could barely contain myself. I wasn't capable of orgasm—at least the mature male orgasm that I know of today—but I would have the equivalent of a female orgasm—where the body vibrates for some time like a tuning fork that's been struck. I would bring the new sneakers home, lock myself in my room, and for hours my hands would examine, like a crazed connoisseur, the unmarked soles—and all the while I'd be tingling madly.

Over the months to come, I would continue to erotically examine and touch the soles, watching them as they degraded over time, their little crevices and swishes and jagged edges reduced to smooth flat rubber that was very pleasing to caress.

When I would first get a new pair of sneakers, I would also passionately sniff at them, intoxicating myself with the perfume of the new rubber. Another thing I did is that I would respectfully keep my sneakers, for the first week or so, in their box—they were too new and precious to just be casually left on the floor when I took them off. And when I went to sleep at night, I would put the box by my bed, with the top off, like a coffin at a Catholic wake. I left the box open so that even as I slept I could breathe in the sneakers' fragrance, which only lasted a few days. Also, I liked to stare at my sneakers right up until the point I passed out—my night-light providing just enough illumination.

Why was I so into sneakers? Well, there was, obviously, the tactile part: I loved the rubber, the *feel* of the rubber. Why this is, I don't know, but I may have been learning how to use my sense of touch, the way we learn what we like to eat by tasting different foods. There was also, as I describe above, that incredible new sneaker smell. And I must have loved that bouquet, because I associated it with the tremendous feeling of hope that came with new sneakers—that with this pair I would run faster, have greater adventures, more fun. Smells, like music, do seem to be keenly linked to memories and feelings.

And, finally, as a last attempt to understand my sneaker love affair, I know that like children today I took my identity from my sneakers, whether, depending on the year, they were Keds or PUMAs or Converse or Adidas (I'm of the pre-Nike generation). So, you see, with my "cool" sneakers, I could face the world. They were both my shield and, if I needed to flee, my means of escape. It is the childhood version of the way adults judge themselves and others by the cars they drive.

But other people didn't perceive my sneakers the way I did. I vividly remember this time in the sixth grade when I was playing basketball—one-on-one—with the best player in my class.

He was a tall, brutish fellow and he was surprised at how well I played—I was a straight-A student—and he jockishly complimented me: "I didn't think you would be good."

But I was surprised by his surprise. I thought he should have noted before we began playing that I was wearing my special Adidas basketball sneakers with their red, white, and blue stripes, and that this should have indicated to him, despite my straight-A reputation, that only a good player would have such sneakers. I even said to him, in response to his backhanded compliment, "But didn't you see my sneakers?"

"What are you talking about?"

"I'm wearing Adidas," I said.

"So what," he said. Then we finished playing and he won, and I have to say that after that I never quite got the same thrill from a new pair of sneakers. It wasn't because I lost the game—he was the best player in my class and much taller than me and I had expected to lose—but because I had learned that my sneakers didn't change what anybody thought about me. Up until that moment, I hadn't known that, and, in fact, had thought the opposite. I thought my sneakers told everybody who I was.

Recently, over twenty-five years later, I crossed paths with the guy I had played basketball with. He still lives in my hometown and we met in a meeting for people with drinking problems. He's still big, and he doesn't have a gut, but he's very filled out and he still has his hair. He does construction. He's a humble ex-jock, working on his drinking problem. I'm bald and a writer, and I'm working on my drinking problem. We've both ended up in the same place. Who would have thought it? The straight-A student and the basketball star. He was happy to see me. We shook hands. He remembered my name. I wanted to ask him if he remembered our one-on-one game, but I was sure he didn't, so I held my tongue. But seeing him again made me think of those Adidas sneakers. I feel like running out and getting a pair. I've heard they've come back into style.

Around this time last year, I developed a serious problem. The relentless round of cocktail parties, fashion shows, and film premieres that constitute New York social life had begun to take its toll. I just didn't have the strength of character to resist the constant peer pressure. To my eternal shame, I gave up drinking.

America is currently going through one of those periodic bouts of repression that punctuate its history. Those pleasures Europeans associate with urban American life—illicit sex, the perfect dry martini, Bolivian marching powder—have been completely pathologized, and anyone caught enjoying them is immediately press-ganged into joining a twelve-step program. The puritans are on the march, and a new spirit of abstinence is sweeping the country.

I first became aware that I had a problem last summer. I began to notice that I couldn't get through an evening without remaining sober. When I woke up on a Sunday morning, I had the distinctly unpleasant experience of being able to remember what I'd done the night before. I even began to drink club soda when I was at home by myself—a sure sign of sobriety.

By the end of the summer, things had gotten so bad that my friend Cromwell felt compelled to take me aside during an evening of merrymaking at Don Hill's.

"Look, Toby," he said, glancing around nervously to make sure no one was listening, "a bunch of us are becoming real concerned about you. You're drinking way, way too little." He downed his shot of tequila and looked at me expectantly. I failed to respond, so he decided to play his trump card. "I didn't want to have to say this," he said, lowering his voice to a whisper, "but I'm beginning to think you might be a teetotaler."

Yikes! There it was: the dreaded "t" word. I quickly came to my senses and drank heavily for the next few days, but it was only a temporary respite in an otherwise relentless downward spiral. In the fall, a group of my former drinking buddies staged an intervention, dragging me off to Hogs & Heifers for a night of revelry. Cromwell even offered to become my "sponsor," babysitting me until I put my life back on track. But it was no good. By the time winter arrived, I was a fully fledged, no-holds-barred, out-of-control nondrinker. For the next six months, my life would be a living hell.

By now, you're familiar with the teetotaler's tale of woe. The nondrinker's memoir has become something of a cliché in New York publishing circles. Malachy McCourt, Caroline Knapp, Dani Shapiro—how much happier they all were before they became victims of the modern temperance movement. They now lead lives of quiet desperation, measuring out their existence in cups of decaf.

My own story is not so very different. Once I'd clambered aboard the wagon, I realized the extent to which my social life had revolved around alcohol. At parties, for instance, my time had been spent finding out what my friends wanted to drink, making my way to the drinks table, pouring the drinks; then making my way back to my friends, carrying the drinks. Now that I was a teetotaler, there really didn't seem to be that much to do at parties.

Even if I did manage to strike up a conversation with someone, they soon tired of me when they discovered I wasn't imbibing. People with a fondness for alcohol are intensely suspicious of nondrinkers. Their attitude is similar to that of Homer Simpson's toward Flanders, his goody-two-shoes next-door neighbor. *So,* they think to themselves, *you think you're better than me, do you? I'll show you, you Bible-bashing, seat belt–wearing, citizenship-award-holding so-and-so, you.* Then they spill red wine all over your clean white trousers.

The awful truth is: You do feel slightly superior to your alcohol-sodden friends. It's difficult not to when they're singing along to "Achy Breaky Heart," or trying to uproot a stop sign. Even if they're not making complete fools of themselves, they're just not as interesting as they are when they're sober. It's hard to laugh at an anecdote when you're hearing it for the fourth time. Then there's the complete absence of sex. As someone who'd been drinking since puberty, I had no idea how to chat up a woman when I was stone-cold sober. My usual tactic had been to get them drunk, then pounce (original, huh?). But it's tough to get a woman drunk if you're not drinking. It's even tougher to pounce. In fact, I didn't even feel like pouncing since my libido had declined dramatically. Drinking reduces you to your animal self. You want to eat, defecate, fight, and fuck. Without alcohol, I turned into an anorexic, constipated, cowardly eunuch.

So I ended up staying in. At first this had its compensations. I caught up on my reading and filed a backlog of expenses. I replied to all my e-mail messages and returned a bunch of calls. I paid all outstanding bills. That took care of about twenty-four hours. Then I started to go mad with boredom. *Seinfeld* six nights a week can drive you nuts after a while, particularly since Channel 11 only shows about a dozen episodes which it plays over and over again.

Fortunately, I managed to avoid joining Alcoholics Anonymous. I've never understood the whole AA movement. Why would a decent, upstanding alcoholic wish to remain anonymous? It was wretched teetotalers like me who should be ashamed of themselves.

Gradually, miraculously, I began to recover. Admittedly, it was slow going at first—a bottle of Amstel Lite here, a white-wine spritzer there—but I wasn't about to give up. It takes hard work, self-discipline, and a lot of good, old-fashioned stick-to-it-ness to become an alcoholic. If you end up back on the wagon, the important thing is to fall right off again.

By this summer, things were almost back to normal. My nights were spent in a glorious haze of being rude to strangers, falling over a lot and waking up at dawn, lying fully clothed on my living room floor with the stereo blasting away at full volume. I was beginning to feel like my old self again.

Of course, I suffer from the occasional relapse. I went through an intense bout of self-loathing after one particularly drunken night on Shelter Island during which I was banned for life from a bar called The Dory for slapping the sixty-four-year-old proprietress on the bum. After that, I couldn't drink for, oh, at least forty-eight hours. It was miserable, particularly because it came after 105 consecutive nights of drunkenness. I had to start all over again after that. As my friend Cromwell says, "One day at a time, Toby. One day at a time."

Wrapping with Christo

DANA VACHON

As I settled into a sofa on the second floor of Christo's and Jeanne Claude's Howard Street studio in New York City, I felt panic—I was about to interview the world's most famous artist team. They've worked together for over half a century, draping and wrapping synthetic fibers over and around Colorado valleys, California hills, Germany's Reichstag, Paris's Pont Neuf, and this coming winter, New York's Central Park. Like their work, Christo and Jeanne Claude are huge. While I was nervously awaiting a sign to begin my interview, Jeanne Claude's freshly dyed hair towered up into the air, burning bright and red like my anxious blood. I spotted a pay phone across the studio and thought to run to it, and call someone for help. Alas, this phone would be of little use to me— like so much else in the studio, it had been wrapped. I switched on my recorder, and we began to talk.

Jeanne Claude: What is it that we want to create? We wish to create works of art, and joy and beauty, which have essentially no purpose whatsoever. They are good for nothing, except to be a work of art, and that is what every true artist does. . . . And like every true artist, like everyone who is truly an artist, we create them for us, and our friends, not for the public. If people like it, it is only a bonus.

Christo: This is one of the reasons we don't do commissions.

JC: That is why we don't accept sponsors.

Dana Vachon: Even if a sponsor came to you with a million dollars?

C: A million! Several come with a million dollars!

DV: How about if a sponsor came to you with a billion dollars? No?

JC: It's very simple. When someone says, "I want to write your charity a check," we say we don't accept it, but if you choose to purchase a work of art, if you have no use for them you can give it to a museum.

DV: What if someone came to you with a gillion dollars?

JC: We don't have enough work for a gillion dollars.

DV: A gillion dollars is a lot of money, no?

JC: Not even for a billion dollars. For four hundred million dollars we can sell all our storages . . .

DV: You've worked on the West Coast. Now you work on the East Coast. Do you consider yourself to be primarily West Coast wrappers or East Coast wrappers?

JC: Okay. First, we have never wrapped anything on the West Coast. *The Running Fence* had nothing to do with wrapping. In the Midwest, *The Valley Curtain* had nothing to do with wrapping. *The Umbrellas* had nothing to do with wrapping. You understand this? *Surrounded Island*s had nothing to do with wrapping.

C: You see very well that the islands, the fabric was floating on the surface of the water.

DV: So, you wrap when you want to wrap; otherwise it's freestyle.

C: Of course! Of course!

DV: Interesting. Jay-Z is another artist who matters a lot today. He is a famous rapper in New York. But he said, "I'm going to leave rapping behind." Have you ever had that impulse?

JC: The last time in our life that we had a wish to wrap something was in 1975. *1975.* Were you born then?

DV: I was not. I was perhaps in the womb. . . .

JC: And that wish was to wrap the Pont Neuf in Paris. It took us ten years to get permission, but that was our last wish to create the work of art based on wrapping. Even the Reichstag, the idea came, we started it in

1971. Until 1975 we never had an idea involving wrapping. Because we do work with ideas that come out of our hearts and our heads, never other people's ideas. And once a project has been refused we have the choice—either we persist as we did for the ones Christo just mentioned, or we lose interest, it is no longer in our heart, and since we do the work for us, why on earth should we do it?

DV: Sure, and that's why you won't take a gillion dollars—because it's the art. . . .

C [*Struggling*]: No. . . .

JC: No. No. No. We wouldn't take a zillion dollars because we don't have enough work to sell for a zillion dollars. . . .

DV: A zillion?

JC: A zillion is more than a billion.

DV: And a gillion, to be sure.

C: Now, the money is big issue. Is difficult, but is not impossible. The most difficult part is the permits.

DV: Sure. And you guys do that together, and one of the stories of your art and the story of Christo and Jeanne Claude is the team. So, this is a question that, if you could forgive my thought, but, sort of for Christo and then Jeanne Claude: When Christo met Jeanne Claude, right—before Jeanne Claude and Christo were "Jeanne Claude and Christo. . . . "

JC [*Interrupting*]: Christo and Jeanne Claude.

C: Christo and Jeanne Claude.

DV: Christo and Jeanne Claude.

C: Yeah.

DV: And maybe even before Christo became "Christo."

C: Ah-hah.

DV: Looking at Jeanne-Claude, did Christo know this was the partner, this was the person who would become Jeanne Claude Christo?

JC [*Laughing*]: No! No! No! We were twenty-three years old, and he was a great lover and still is, and that's it!

DV: When I say, "curtain," what comes to mind?

JC: Valley.

C: Valley.

DV: When I say, "umbrella," what comes to mind?

JC: Blue in Japan. Yellow in California.

DV: Let me ask you one last: "Zeitgeist."

JC: Who?

DV: "Zeitgeist."

Christo [*To JC*]: That's a German word.

JC: What is *Zeitgeist*?

DV: It's the spirit of the times.

C: Yeah. German. German word.

DV: I'm trying to get behind the process of the inspiration.

C: How were we inspired for each project? It's not general idea. It's all something. . . .

JC: Let's talk about our experiences. Our experiences are different for each project. . . . The process leading toward the completion, the process is very important, but it is not the aim. The aim is to see *The Gates in Central Park* in February. That is the aim. On human terms it is very much the same as a nine-month pregnancy for a woman. That is not the aim. The aim is that one day she will finally see the baby!

DV: So, the baby is Picasso?

C: No, the project! No, the project! The project! The project!

JC: The baby is the project!

C: The project!

DV: So the baby is Calder?

C: The project. *The Gates.* The baby is *Reichstag.* The baby is *Running Fence.* The baby is *Valley Curtain.* Each project is like a child of ours.

JC [*Pointing to a postcard of a painting by Giotto*]: Now, something else about art history, why we like to do fabric, because for over five thousand years artists have been fascinated with fabric, forming folds, pleats, and draperies. This is Giotto. . . .

DV: Giotto.

JC: You see how much fabric there is, and how just a few small faces?

DV: Cimabue taught Giotto, correct?

C: Yeah. But Giotto has more fabric than Cimabue. . . .

DV: Now, Cimabue taught Giotto. Who is your Giotto?

JC: Giotto is our Giotto!

DV: No. *You're* Cimabue. Who is *your* Giotto?

C: No, no, no. For us, our Giotto is Giotto.

DV: But I'm saying, if *you're* Cimabue, who is *your* Giotto?

C: Okay. If we're Cimabue . . . ?

JC: Why should we be Cimabue?

C: We're Christo! And Giotto, is Giotto.

Sticky Feet

BILL POWERS

In my defense, I would like to quote Pola Wise, a former Next model, who once told me that the most romantic thing anyone had ever done on her behalf was "fly cross country and stalk me." She had confirmed what every lustful red-blooded American boy—including myself—dared to suspect: that, yes, amorous longings coupled with a fierce determination could very well triumph over a wavering lover's heart.

After all, was Romeo anything more than just another silver-tongued stalker loitering around some fair maiden's backyard? Who didn't silently cheer during that famous scene from *The Graduate* when Dustin Hoffman wins Katherine Ross's hand in happiness as he almost psychotically steals her away from the altar? This joyous reunion only occurred because, against the odds, Ben had followed his lost love to Berkeley, where she was enrolled in university.

I, too, thought my vagaries were chivalrous at the time. Lonely and broken, holding court on an East Village stoop across from my ex-girlfriend's apartment, I waited impatiently for her to come around, in more ways than one. While on occasion I questioned the depravity of my incessant tracking, the reasoning behind it always seemed, in my mind, utterly sound. If her contention, her justification for abandoning our bond, somehow stemmed from a perceived lack of loyalty or commitment on my part, then I was there, uninvited, proving otherwise. And should my efforts bear nothing but self-torment, then I could move on confident that the failed coupling had not sprung from my equivocal acceptance of her dismissal. Of course, to me, the idea of a gorgeous, witty, trust-fund fortified twenty-three-year-old forsaking the opportunity to share in my life of squalor and disappointment seemed entirely implausible.

Alas, some months passed. My friends tried convincing me that if I took an honest appraisal of previous love affairs was there even a one over which I still harbored a resentment? Had they not all ended for the best? Could I name a single girl who, in retrospect, I truly didn't want to live without? Begrudgingly, I confessed that "no" I could not recall a woman who had ever scratched such an indelible mark on my love line. My confidantes then argued that surely this was proof enough to clear away any meandering doubts from my clouded thinking. They suggested the only thing left to do was "forget that bitch" and jump back into the downtown dating pool. And yet their insistence only proved to reinforce my twisted perception. In pointing out how many preceding romances had essentially boiled down to a series of extended one-night stands, I became absolutely resolute in my belief that this interminable love for my current ex, who'd been recently tapped to model in a DKNY campaign, wasn't just your typical male obsession rooted on some superficial physical plane. No, it was nothing short of destiny that we grow old together.

Obviously, I told no one of my all-night vigils on East Ninth Street, gazing up at my girl's second-story window for shadows dancing off her rice-paper shades. I spoke not a word of the hours I wasted following her nightly rituals from afar—the way the room glowed blue as she caught a repeat of *Law & Order* or an old *Seinfeld* episode. However, creepy and pathetic it might seem, these stakeouts were of vital importance. I needed to know that she still walked in the world and being around her allayed my desperate sense of isolation.

Now for the record, I never carried a Thermos or constructed notes out of yesterday's newspaper like "I'lL TeAch yOu How tO love mE." At worst, I was a nuisance, although I'm certain a restraining order against me wouldn't have been too hard to secure. Like most outbursts of deviance, the big question I ask myself today is: Why did I do it? A rational mind—a normal person if you will—would have quickly deduced that this absurd journey of mine was simply a cul-de-sac of misery. But I recalled what mentors and family patriarchs had embalmed in me as a teen, the fact that 90 percent of all successful business ventures could be chalked off to persistence.

Unfortunately, my last-ditch efforts did not pan out like some convenient third act in a Hugh Grant comedy. So after sixteen weeks of torment, my obsessive-compulsive behavior began a steady slide into remission. The phone calls just to hear the outgoing message on her voicemail trickled off. I mapped out alternate routes if I was required to enter the East Village so as *not* to pass her apartment building. The pain of phantom love eventually outweighed the hardship of having to concede all hope was lost. On occasion I still missed her, but at the same time understood my proclivity for whitewashing personal history. Now I laugh on those random nights I find myself driving down her block and catch a glimpse through that yonder window, a reflection from a life I was not meant to be a part of.

Matthew Barney vs. Jeff Koons

Matthew Barney: I don't feel that I'm able to find sculpture in galleries very often, and I feel I can always find that in what you do; I can always find an essential belief in the object in your work.

Jeff Koons: As an artist the only thing that I know how to do is to trust in myself and to follow my interests, and hope that they take me to some kind of archetypal area, so that I am dealing with images that—hopefully—are communal, and have a sense of importance to society; that it's not about the self, but that the vocabulary is really a collective vocabulary.

MB: I think that the way you arrive at the forms, and particularly the way you make them requires so much belief—belief in the materials, belief in the surfaces, trusting that these physical qualities can have enough resonance to carry the work. Maybe that's a common value that we have; I think if someone doesn't make things they don't understand what it takes to arrive at something like one of your pieces.

JK: What's really great in art is the physicality that it can have, the strength of a color, how pink a pink can be, how turquoise a turquoise can be, how a certain sensual quality can express itself. All those things lead to very physical responses, so I think it's always so interesting, these things that are anchored in really subjective areas, such as the chemical response of the viewers, but at the same time open the vocabulary.

MB: As artists we're always put in this position, in interviews and conversations with the outside world, about the meaning, and about these things as images, but I think that the path that you have to follow to get these things up and standing on their own in the real world is certainly as meaningful as any narrative behind it.

JK: The narrative to me really seems like icing on the cake. If you really focus on your interests and follow them, the narrative comes and sugar-coats everything.

MB: Maybe the word I'm searching for is presence, which is probably an old-fashioned way of thinking about sculpture, but I think for me that's how I relate to what you do. You walk into a room and there's an object there and it has an incredible presence, and it's not an image at all. You've got to walk around this thing to understand it; it's a challenging, physical *thing*.

JK: A lot of time if you have an idea and you don't execute it, it's really like a rung on a ladder, in that it dematerializes, and the possibility of the type of escape that you have—into really being able to take your work somewhere—is lost. One of the things about art and the process I go through every day when I come to the studio is the removal of anxiety. And that process is one that just lets you make a gesture, because the only thing that holds you back from gesture is anxiety.

People often ask me if I have any interest in film, and film is something that really, in a way, I've been terrified of. I played with the idea, years ago, of making a film, but I knew that I really wasn't going to do it—the medium in itself really seems a little overwhelming to me.

MB: I don't use film, I use video, so it's quite different, but for me the lead weight of making a motion picture is that you have to sustain energy over a very long period of time, and I think it's different from sustaining energy along the production of an object. I guess it's because of all the active egos that go into making a film—that brand of collaboration and keeping that level of energy up for that long. I'd say that's the toughest part.

BlackBook: You both seem very private people, but I wonder how much confession and biography can be read into your work, and whether that's something you encourage.

JK: When I drive to work sometimes I like to listen to songs in the car. There's one song I've been enjoying recently, which is Led Zeppelin's "Since I've Been Loving You," and it's a live version, and they're playing in California, and it is so moving, and it is such a testimony, and it's, like, "This is really how powerful art can be," and it is a testimonial. Personally, I don't like it when things become about the self, but I think you have to have something anchored in personal iconography. If you're not anchored there, you can't go to this other pole. There's kind of a polarity between personal iconography and mass iconography.

MB: In the sense that you become the conductor between those two.

JK: I remember in the late seventies I made a couple of pieces, inflatable flowers and an inflatable rabbit, and I stopped making that work because I thought it revealed too much about myself, just the colors, these bright blues, these bright pinks, these bright greens—sexually it was *so* charged up, I thought, "Oh this is too revealing." Revealing of what? I don't know—just strong sexuality. So I went on and made *The New* [a series of cleaning appliances in sterile, illuminated showcases] which is more removed.

MB: I think at a certain point with *The Cremaster Cycle* I felt comfortable to identify it as a self-portrait, but I think that when I'm making things, I don't think about it in those terms. Maybe it has something to do with having a certain addiction to abstraction, to distance, craving that from things in the world, and wanting to make things that function that way so that by the time something becomes an object it's transformed so many times that it doesn't have my face on it anymore. That said, I think I am more willing these days to identify what I have done as autobiographical in terms of its overall arc.

BlackBook: What does "all-American" mean to you?

MB: In spite of the last couple of years I think I still have a romantic notion of what the American spirit is in terms of making things, and it's something to do with the privilege of not having as much of a historical burden; we're raised in a culture that doesn't have much of an art history. I feel like I could still identify an American spirit in certain ways of art making.

JK: And a sense of avant-garde. I think young American artists' sense of what it means to be young and avant-garde is very different—a European would probably think they have to make something that also stands up to other things; it's not just for what it is, on its own.

MB: Art in America has never been a primary carrier of cultural information the way the painting tradition was in Europe at one point, and I think there's something liberating about that.

BlackBook: Does art have a relationship to what's happening in the world?

MB: Totally, but I feel that what keeps me excited about art that I'm seeing is that it has the ability to distill the world around it in a much more refined way than I think anything else can. Painting can't be what it used to be, as the primary carrier of the cultural narrative— I mean, we've got television, we've got movies, we've got all these things that do that in a much more efficient way—but I think that nothing can touch what art can do in terms of really refining something to the essence, and that goes for distilling the external world around us, or distilling the essence of who the artist is—whatever it is it's still very exciting to me, and totally relevant and necessary.

JK: Art deals with things, but it doesn't deal with things so specifically that it becomes meaningless, and that gives it the ability to be chameleon enough to exist in the next moment, because if something is so specific about this moment, and not really about much broader things, it can't function in the next moment.

MB: I was going to ask you, Jeff, how are you feeling about New York? Does it still feel as exciting to be here?

JK: I love it, because information is so accessible, and I'm interested in art as a vehicle and an energy, and I want to be in the trenches with the kids that are just moving here.

MB: I feel the same; this is such a small place geographically that you can't not be in the trenches, which is great. Do you go to other cities and feel like there's more of a sense of community among artists?

JK: No, I think it's pretty amazing here, and maybe you can go to communities that are smaller—I like to go to Germany—but in terms of art, in a sense, as a community, and seeing exhibitions, I really like it here.

MB: I love it here, but I have to say I miss the mountains where I grew up in Idaho. There's a purging that happens for me when I go up in elevation—a kind of clarity that's hard to find here.

JK: I'm always amazed by the different types of dirt. So you go to a restaurant that's outside the city, maybe three or more hours outside the city; you start to see that there's a different type of dirt—it's still dirt, but it's just different.

BlackBook: Matthew, you worked as a model for a while.

MB: For five years, through college. Hell of a good job. I learned a lot about being on a set. I also think that at a certain point, after being inside someone else's narrative over and over again, and not feeling particularly connected to it, I guess you learn how malleable you are as a vessel—you can carry all these different stories. Having never done any acting of any sort it was a surprise to me—that I could despise something and represent it simultaneously.

JK: From the time that I was a child I was always involved in sales, whether it was going door-to-door selling candy, gift-wrapping paper, or selling soft drinks on a golf course; but it was always a way that I felt I was meeting people's needs. It wasn't just a one-way street, that I was selling somebody something: I was going door-to-door, and you know every home is different; in a way it was a beginning, to me, of an accep-tance of people, and the differences between people. Did modeling give you . . . it must have given you a sense of confidence in yourself?

MB: Sure, there's no end to the amount of reinforcement you get in that position, which, of course, is problem-atic. Where the equation starts to go sour is where you fear that you're actually giving more of your self away with these images than you first believed.

BlackBook: Are you able to keep finding new ways to be inspired, or do you even need to?

MB: Once your language becomes developed, it becomes the filter through which you try to understand the world, really. The only way I can read a book is if it has something to do with what's within the radar of my project as an artist at that moment. I can't deviate from that scope.

JK: It's this constant thing of always taking all the belief in what you're doing and dismantling it and trying to look at everything completely fresh again.

MB: I feel that what I do is a hell of a lot of hard work and a lot of effort, and when I think about artists who have continued, over time, to come back each time and hit the nail on the head, but each time they come back to the nail there's less effort involved in hitting it, those are the really inspiring examples, where the gesture becomes more and more effortless. I personally feel that I'm nowhere close to that; I feel there's *so* much effort exerted in what I do, and so much . . . *work*.

JK: Economy, the appreciation of economy. That's what's so great in Andy's [Warhol] work. It's like in energy systems—people are always looking to find ways in which less is used to create more.

MB: Hey, Jeff, I've got a question for you. You've spent a lot of time in Germany; do you think you could define the difference between the American deer hunt and the German deer hunt? I mean, in relation to the landscape—the relationship the hunter has to the landscape; it's something I've always wondered about, and I can't define it.

JK: What's interesting in looking at the landscape is that you notice the little shed where people will sit to spot deer and to really follow their habits, or to wait for them, and also just the scale of the European deer is smaller, and I guess the combination of these two things—how you follow the routine of the deer, and also their scale would affect something within that hunt.

MB: Was there a lot of hunting around York where you grew up?

JK: I went deer hunting only one time, and I didn't have a proper rifle—I ended up having just a shotgun with gloves. [*Matthew laughs.*] So I probably wouldn't have had much luck even if one had walked right in front of me. But it's interesting, all my friends would go, and at that time of year, hunting season, school would almost just come to a standstill.

MB: Same in Idaho—half of our football team would leave; it was right in the middle of football season. There's something in that, for me anyway, something to do with the way you own or don't own the landscape, and I think there might be an American tendency to feel like you don't own the landscape, and that's maybe handed down from just a handful of generations of exploring it, and still not really knowing all of it.

BlackBook: Andy Warhol personified the artist-as-celebrity, which is something you've both experienced. How did you feel when you realized you were heading toward celebrity status yourselves?

JK: I think sometimes it's looked at a little bit as a tool—that for the service of your work it's important that people are aware that you're doing your work, but it has to really be balanced, because at the same time you need the intimacy with your work, of not having distraction, and being able to focus specifically on the work, and that's one of the great luxuries that artists have, that you don't at every moment have to be maintaining a presence. I always think of that "Got Milk?" commercial, all these celebrities being photographed with the milk on their lip—we don't have to do that.

MB: I think that we're all trying to create a language that communicates, and so having a more direct interface with the world is helpful in that way. The other side of the knife is that if a form becomes overexposed it loses resonance. It may gain resonance as an image, but I believe it loses resonance as a form, and it's something I try to protect when I choose to participate, or not participate, in the media.

JK: For me it's really about the service of the work; generally, if I'm involved in some form of media where I have to speak, I'm not ever really happy with the experience, because art's also a transcendence, it's really about *becoming* instead of defining what you are or what you've been.

MB: Yeah, right, you make a visual language for that reason— that's the best way you can communicate, so it's ironic to end up being in a situation like this where you are having to talk about this stuff, which often feels completely useless. Being involved in this conversation, though, is a much different situation than appearing in a magazine. In other words, the idea of having a conversation with Jeff is appealing, whereas often the idea of being featured in a magazine feels like you're part of that machine of selling magazines, and that always feels a bit uncomfortable to me.

BlackBook: It would be hard to leave this conversation without talking about sex. Are viewers right to spend so much time noticing the sex in your work?

JK: Of the tools that artists have to work with, sex is one of the most powerful, and sex is about the survival of the species, so it's a really important part of our existence, and our being, so it's something that just, naturally, I feel wants to be discussed communally.

MB: I think I arrive at my erotic content by thinking so much about process, and thinking about where my own creative process comes from, and my desire to make things, and how I can continue to find that desire, and I think that sort of meditation translates into sexual, and often autoerotic forms. So it feels very central—eroticism—for me.

JK: Just the process of art, of finding metaphor in archetype, sexuality is at the core of things being discussed in a profound way, which is a vehicle to some form of transcendence, of more knowledge. I don't think it's an end-all about sex, but it's some form of lubrication. Matthew, that's a perfect term for you.

Reef or Madness?

NEAL POLLACK

On a steamy, diaphanous afternoon in August 1998, Ernesto Morales, the forty-eight-year-old captain of the New York Diving Department, plunged into what an ordinary diver would consider starkly alienating, even boring, waters—the Hudson River just off Chelsea Piers. For Morales, this was a routine clock punch. He was planning to examine the wreckage of a Lebanaese tugboat that had sunk in 1974, and, if he had time, he thought he might make a quick sweep of the area for loose medical waste. He said later that he had hoped to finish within an hour so he could get home in time to fix himself a ham sandwich and watch the Yankees game.

But halfway though the dive, Morales, for reasons he says he still can't explain, decided to veer a few hundred yards away from his mission. In a radio transmission to his onshore lieutenant, he said, "I'm gonna go down there and see what I can see."

At first, Morales assumed that the colors he spotted were an optical trick, the glint of late-day sunlight of a sheet of sunken metal. But as he went deeper, it became obvious that something else lay beneath the still surface of the Hudson. In some spots, the river floor seemed to glisten blue, glow yellow—a magnificent Swedish flag of color. Morales spotted sharp patches of purple ridged by orange tints; he had only seen colors like this underwater once before, when he visited the Caribbean on his third honeymoon, in 1982. Then, seemingly from out of nowhere, a magnificent blue and white fish rocketed past him, parted the water above, disappeared, and then plunged back in at nearly the exact same spot.

His initial shock at seeing a flying fish soon turned into a somber recognition. Like all good public servants would have, Morales quickly realized that he had a new duty to uphold. "Oh my God," he said to himself. "This is a fucking coral reef. The Hudson is alive."

The decline of coral reefs worldwide has been well documented, at least by scientists. More than a quarter of our reefs are already dead or bleached beyond saving; many others are in jeopardy, and those that are not can hardly be considered top tier. Global climate change is the main culprit, as it is for so many things. The small plants—zooxanthellae—that inhabit coral reefs cannot survive sea temperatures above thirty degrees Celsius, especially when that exposure is accompanied by Latin American pop music. Once these plants are expelled from the reefs, or at least suspended, the corals inside them quickly perish, and reef erosion ensues.

But as the Southern Hemisphere overheats, the Northern Hemisphere becomes merely temperate. While this development, regrettably, hasn't much changed contemporary sexual mores or helped reduce the occurrence of obesity in children, it has created a natural opportunity, and perhaps even a miraculous one. What if, even as global warming is killing our saltwater reefs, it is simultaneously brewing a phenomenon just as incredible: freshwater river reefs? Studies show that the average surface temperature of the Hudson has risen three degrees in the last five years, growing faster than the salary of the average American worker. The reefs that Morales claims to have come upon may prove to be the most important environmental discovery of the last one hundred years. When I call Malcom Mars-Jones, head of the Urban Reef Study Center in Leeds, England, he tells me, "Conceivably, this could forever change the way human beings interact with the environment. Hopefully, it will also improve the quality of British food."

But, naturally, Morales's discovery has its detractors. "Pure nonsense," says Carla Petrocelli, the chief biologist at the National Institute on Global Warming Studies, when I visit her in her office at Annapolis, Maryland. "Global warming is an unnatural, destructive process and it has no positive side effects. And, yes," she adds, "I would like to sleep with you."

The press reaction has been mixed but nonetheless amusing for semiprofessional observers of shifting political alliances. For instance, the archreactionary *New York Post*, in an editorial, wrote that "[Morales] has Love Canal–style panic peddlers running for cover," while the pro-environment *New York Times* called for "a careful study" of "this alleged finding" that could have "serious" implications for "democracy." The BBC interviewed Morales, leading to offers for him to dive the Liffey, the Seine, and the Nile. *Der Spiegel*, the German newsweekly, said, "This American diver should be hailed as a national hero. Instead, he is mostly ignored, because Americans are ignorant."

Captain Morales, at the center of this controversy, has weathered more turbulent storms. His 1990 appointment to head the New York Diving Department was met by howls of protest from the rank and file. Formed to look for evidence of German submarines during World War II, the NYDD was a source of great pride for the Irish Americans who traditionally joined its ranks, as evidenced by their annual float in the St. Patrick's Day Parade, with the proud divers wearing their wetsuits and waving from atop a papier-mâché submarine. A Puerto Rican captain was, to their minds, unacceptable.

But Morales quickly won allies. He purchased high-grade oxygen for his diver's tanks that, according to one officer, "made us feel pretty loopy." He dismissed a corrupt diver who was selling government-issue flippers on the black market. And, at the end of the day, he was the best damn diver the department had ever seen. Said one retired officer, "He cuts through the water like a steak knife through butter."

I met with Morales on a recent afternoon at his home in the Bronx. His current wife, Roberta, was away on a human rights mission, he said, bringing unpopped popcorn to a poor rural region of Ecuador. They have two children, both of whom went to a soul music–appreciation camp for the summer.

"I am confident that I am superior at my work," he told me. "Diving is in my bones and failure is not. When I am below the surface of the Hudson, I'm in control of . . . myself, I guess, and sometimes I feel that I'm in control of nature, too."

He opened a desk drawer and pulled out what appeared to be a piece of coral.

"This is a piece of coral," he said. "It's from the Hudson. Tomorrow, you dive with me, and you will see."

We began our dive at 1:30 p.m., when, Morales says, the sunlight is at its sharpest above the river. For the first twenty minutes or so, all I saw were discarded David Dinkins campaign buttons and the occasional catfish, but the captain urged me on. Suddenly, to my left I spotted a flowery shock of purple, which I later discovered was a colony of rare hydrocorals. That was the first sign. Quickly following were a frosty blue-white family of white stinging sea ferns and organ-pipe corals and the unusual-looking rare-book corals, usually only seen on the North African coast. For the next two hours, Morales and I feasted on the fecundity of the Hudson's depths. We saw anchor, honeycomb, and mushroom corals living alongside one another. Under a pipe we found a colony of impressive bright green brain corals and slightly less impressive brown spleen corals. There were all manner of anemones and zoanthids, and there was even a family of rare speckled flat worms that rose in unison as we passed, as though they were singing a song of discovery. By the time we were done, I could have no more doubts.

Afterward, over scotch at a downtown bar followed by lacrosse fans, Morales expounded on his discovery. Thus far, he said, his pleas for research grants had been dismissed by the Giuliani administration and by Christine Todd Whitman, former governor of New Jersey and head of the Environmental

Protection Agency. But as the story continues to grow, he says, the Hudson's coral reef will become impossible to ignore. "If this is happening here," he said, "then I bet there are reefs growing in urban rivers all over the world. The Volga, the Tiber, the Thames, even maybe the Danube, once they clean up all that pollution—the possibilities are endless."

He sighed and ordered another round.

"Maybe I need to go stage a sit-in at the EPA's office. Maybe then they'll listen."

"It will not work, Ernesto," I said.

"I know," he said. "But I have to try. There are coral reefs growing in the Hudson, I swear. Someday everyone will know."

The day after diving with Morales, I returned to the banks of the river and I knew my time for duty had arrived. So now, with bold heart and bolder mind, I sent this article, this message in a bottle down the river of time into the void. Maybe then Ernesto's nugget of truth will reach whom it must.

The Big Sell

MIKE ALBO

Our stars look like ads, our songs sound like jingles, and our imagery is bright and invasive. Is it any wonder that our brains find it increasingly hard to distinguish between Britney and Pepsi?

Funny, but just the other day I became a product whore. I was writing copy for the smoothie franchise Jamba Juice, which is introducing new locations in Manhattan. They wanted to send fun, snappy letters to hotel concierges, fashion editors, and personal trainers (people they considered "influencers") who would create buzz and help turn their product popular and profitable. Along with the letter, each influencer received loads of free Jamba coupons to hand out to his or her well-appointed tastemaker friends. As part of my payment, I got the coupons too.

Pretty soon I was handing out those fuckers like nobody's business. The power of bestowing upon my friends a free smoothie gave me a populist Johnny Appleseed thrill. I would see cronies and colleagues and slip them a free smoothie with a smile. The brightly colored coupons became the friendly capper to any conversation—"Hey, have a free Jamba Juice! It's the pizza slice of the new millennium! Talk to you later!"

But you must be used to this kind of stuff. As a savvy reader of *BlackBook*, you are probably a demographic that marketers cream their distressed jeans over—doing anything they can to get your cool-kid stamp of approval for one of the estimated two million products launched every year into our already clogged consumer atmosphere.

But for me it was like I had superpowers. Within a week's time, I became one of those weird hypesters you may have read about—people employed by new, extremely successful firms with names like BzzAgents or Tremor to turn their friends on to Clairol hair color or Valvoline Oil by just casually bringing it up in conversation and handing out free samples.

What scares me is that I had absolutely no problem doing it and I would do it again, because I actually love Jamba Juice, no joke. Or did it make me love it? It's hard to tell the difference these days.

My Jambagasm is but another example of our current state of constant marketing. From the rise of hypesters to recent studies on how advertising affects the brain to the gaudy, logo-laden look of our celebrities, this year it has become more obvious than ever: Those shiny brands intend to insinuate themselves into almost every crack and crevice of our lives, including our minds, and there is no turning back.

Each time commercial efforts seem satisfied with their presence, a sliver of previously ad-free space gets turned into a pop opportunity. Time and time again, I am freshly startled at the creative new ways that advertising shows up in my daily routine. E-mails are being "data-mined," airline seats are rigged with telescreens, coffee cozees are covered with ads, your laptop is scattered with pop-ups, and now I have become a human sandwich board for a smoothie. In fact, just this month a patent was approved for a new toothbrush that transmits music right into your mouth while you brush your teeth.

Nowhere is this acceptable relentlessness more apparent than in the entertainment industry. Branding has invaded television shows, video games, movies, and novels to such an extent that it's no longer scandalous. A simple night out at a Cineplex, for example, has become a major ordeal—you have to sit and stare at ten minutes of loud visually arresting commercials before even the trailer starts (which is not only irritating, but really screws up the delicate timing of your pot buzz). Then you sit there for the feature, like last season's straight-to–Jet Blue masterpiece *In Good Company*, and watch Topher Grace talk into his Starbucks or Scarlet Johannsen fingering a slice of Domino's pizza and try your best to feel a private emotion.

Branding seems to have reached the very root of our entertainment culture, which is pretty much all of culture these days.

Just look at our stars—always a good litmus test of the times. They have become preened, depilated alien lifeforms saturated in brands—geared up with their Coach spots and iPod appearances, mouthing, "It's Versace," to photographers, and then leaving their premieres and awards shows piled high with gift bags full of Sprayology products and certificates for free Lasik surgery (that was really an item in the Tony Awards bag last year!). Our stars have become indelibly linked to their sponsors. I see Hilary Swank, and suddenly Calvin Klein underwear is dangled in front of my face.

Our stars look like ads, our songs sound like jingles, and our imagery is bright and invasive. It's difficult these days to listen to a piece of music or look at an image without imagining its present or future commercial self. Now you can't even "Pull into Nazareth . . ." without aching to switch your cellular coverage to Cingular. When Gwen sings "If I Were a Rich Girl," you start salivating for a Pepsi. And watch out—it's probably safe to assume that J. Lo already has licensed her new album, *Rebirth*, to at least fifteen brand tie-ins. When you hear her dancebeat singles, I promise you will start feeling urges for some products you haven't even heard of yet. Even the past has been mined—with dead singers like Elvis and Marilyn Monroe appearing in commercial efforts.

Of course we've been living with product placement for years now—or at least since Drew and ET shared some Reeses Pieces. But nowadays, it's common for products to be flung in front of our faces. We've accepted the constant barrage the same way we accept acid rain and code orange alerts—they are just another part of our days and nights, having reached into us so deeply that we don't even notice the numbing botoxic effects upon our soul.

If you don't think that all this brand dancing hasn't deeply affected you on a cellular level, you should check out the recently published scientific studies that purportedly show how brands and marketing actually cause notable brain activity, and, possibly, permanent influence.

This new field, called neuromarketing, uses MRI scanners and other brain-imaging machines common in the work of cognitive neuroscience to study the reaction of the brain to certain cultural images. The repercussions are pretty skeevy; brands may have a way of imprinting upon the brain.

Read Montague of Baylor University applied MRI technology to the "Pepsi Challenge." He monitored subjects when they drank Coke and Pepsi in blind taste tests and then again when they drank it knowing the brand beforehand—finding that Coke, above all, caused high amounts of activity in the part of the brain associated not just with memory and recall, but with self-image. In other words, when people *knew* they were drinking Coke they rated it more highly.

Another study by the ominously named "Brighthouse Neurotechnologies Group" hooked viewers up to brain scanners, and registered their reactions to a mix of familiar logos and famous people along with more mundane imagery. Blood flow was again heightened in the brain's prefrontal cortex when seeing modern icons like Madonna, Coke, Bill Clinton, and Ford trucks.

These experiments suggest two things—that the brain reacts to brands on an emotional level, and that famous people are like brands. Coke and Madonna both cause the brain to flood with blood in the same way as when you see your mom, or remember that time you were bullied in junior high, or recall your first orgasmic love. And if this is remotely true, it starts to make sense why our stars have been used like psychic Goodyear Blimps to get our attention. And why our stars are beginning to look so flat and vacant and why there are so damn many of them now. They are being used as branders.

Although neuromarketing hasn't really led to anything specific besides trendy MRI conjecture, it's easy to imagine our imagery's becoming more and more arresting and attuned to our brain activity in order to hit that prefrontal cortex g-spot. In fact, that process seems already to be in the works: At the recent Toy Fair in Manhattan, an estimated 70 percent of new toys were interactive. Using microchip and video-encoded invisible light (VEIL) technology, a new breed of wireless toys become activated by receiving digital signals from an encoded TV show. Mattel's new VEIL-enabled Batman action figure and Batmobile will respond to the new Warner Bros. *Batman* series out this fall. While watching the show, the toys can be activated to receive the encoded signal. So the Batmobile toy revs up at the same time that the cartoon car is ready to go on the screen, and the Batman action figure interacts in real time with the cartoon. Give that toy to a child and watch his head explode.

It's like our products are becoming more human, and not just for kids. Online Web sites like Netflix, Amazon, and iTunes have evolved into intuitive best friends who constantly give you suggestions of what else you should be digging—actively "learning" our tastes so they can market "similar" novelists, movies, and musicians to us—literally becoming us, entering our headspace.

It's clear that our "arts and sciences" are now tangled up with commerce to such an extent that there is no turning back. We live in a bubble of conditioned hitmakers—always bouncy, always accessible, always with Clay Aiken–style emotion. Our current landscape of music and imagery is only getting more eye-catching. This accelerated pace takes a lot of work, both for the viewer and for the creators. To keep up the high production value our eyes are addicted to, it's like the entire country is going to have to turn into a Galliano show.

Entertainment itself seems to be experiencing a kind of transduction of the creative spirit; instead of an advertisement attaching itself to a work of art, the ad is becoming the artistic whole. The blurred boundaries between art and commerce is producing a refined, dizzying world around us. What will the future be like? Take a look at kaleidoscopic imagery of motion graphics used in ads for products such as Nike and Bombay Sapphire and imagine that happening *all the time.*

I'm just as freaked out about all this as you may be, but the old ways of retaliation don't seem to be effective. During the WTO protests, rioters in Seattle threw rocks at Starbucks while wearing Levi's and Nikes. And, anyway, the last time people got all anti-establishment, their anger was co-opted and turned into marketable nostalgia in the form of Hippie chic, VH1 shows, and a series of glossy fashion ads.

The real revolution seems to be in the mind. It's like you are being chased in your head for the key to your deepest desires. One way is to be constantly vigilant of your tastes and to stay slippery. The next time some Web site suggests a product you would like, say: "Fuck you! I don't want to buy that Norah Jones album!"

I guess that doesn't seem so revolutionary. I wonder if there is any way to escape. Maybe it's just the next step in human evolution. Do we really want it to go away? I mean, I kind of love Beyoncé. And anyway, I don't think our gooey huge consumer machine is going to slink back into the swamp anytime soon. We have become tolerant of embedded messages and hybrid forms of entertainment. We love Christina Aguilera, read magalogs like *Lucky* and *Cargo*, dream of being *American Idols*. Perhaps we should accept our product-cyborg lives. Let's get neuromarketed!

Maybe when we have become fully integrated with our brands and every flare of our cortexes has been studied, we won't need to use entertainment to advertise, and we can once again enjoy a sponsorless song or work of art. What will happen when the brand world inhabits our bodies? Maybe then we will all be free—or at least get more free stuff.

If Death Is Just a Doorway . . . Why Shouldn't It Have a Door Policy?

CHUCK PALAHNIUK

ARE YOU ON THE LIST?

Imagine yourself at the smartest, most fabulous party in all of recorded history. . . . You: An insider. A VIP. No longer barred by those red-velvet ropes. Imagine practically rubbing elbows with movie stars, business tycoons, brilliant scientists, and the leading artists in music. Thanks to hours of pampering by a top Hollywood stylist, you've never looked better. And now you're sharing the spotlight with celebrities the world will always admire. National leaders. Award-winning writers. Record-setting athletes. All these heroes who've created history. And You.

And the best part is, this wonderful party goes on—forever.

WELCOME TO THE AFTERPARTY

Even if your life has lacked glamour and applause, your death doesn't have to. Welcome to a new concept in memorial care: The AfterParty Lounge. Here, every guest will reside in close proximity with a star. Beyond "until death do us part," wouldn't you love to curl up beside sexy and alluring Angelina Jolie? Or ruggedly handsome Tom Cruise? Your final resting place can be just inches away. In addition, each AfterParty Lounge will feature a full bar with a variety of live music throughout the week. And with AfterParty Lounges opening soon in New York, Miami, Los Angeles, and Seattle, your final home can be a place your children—and their children—will visit often. And with pride.

In short, this can be the most important piece of real estate you'll ever buy.

PUT YOURSELF ON THE LIST

AfterParty guests may choose from three levels of amenities. With each level offering exceptional attention and service.

LEVEL ONE: FEATURED TALENT

Our top level includes the exclusive BodyGuard Service. Every year, dozens of deceased celebrities are sexually abused or portioned out for sale over the Internet. With our BodyGuard Service, you can rest assured your DNA *and* your dignity will remain intact. Plus, our Always & Forever Red Rose Assurance that *you'll receive a fresh long-stemmed American Beauty—EVERY DAY for all eternity.*

LEVEL TWO: INDUSTRY PLAYER

This level includes coveted Insider Eye–Level placement of your crypt, within a guaranteed distance of no more than 6 feet (1.8 meters) from a world-famous celebrity. Your death announcement will be issued press release–style to the three media outlets of your choice, complete with an on-file paparazzi-style headshot. Plus, our exclusive *Searchlight & Red Carpet Arrival for your mourning party.*

LEVEL THREE: ENTOURAGE

Not everyone needs center stage. But this level still keeps you close to the action, with placement no farther than 30 feet (9.2 meters) from a big-name star. And for a limited time—*Up to twenty luxury gift bags of complimentary bath and grooming products for your surviving next of kin.*

R.S.V.P. . . . A.S.A.P.!

As the Baby Boomers age, terrorists run rampant, and sexually transmitted diseases infect millions, you may only control one aspect of your final end. So accept our invitation. Join us as an AfterParty guest. Be there, in the best company, in the spotlight, forever and ever and ever. . . .

The AfterParty Lounge. . . .
With So Many Stars,
You'll Think You're in Heaven!

THE AFTERPARTY GUEST LIST ALREADY INCLUDES*

Anne Rice

Bette Midler

Britney Spears

Catherine Deneuve

Charles Barkley

Cher

Christopher Walken

David Beckham

David Bowie

Dominick Dunne

Donald Trump

Ethan Hawke

Fran Lebowitz

Glenn Close

Irvine Welsh

Joan Rivers

John McEnroe

Kevin Bacon

Linda Evangelista

Martha Stewart

Maya Angelou

Mel Gibson

Nelson Mandela

Nicole Kidman

Oprah Winfrey

Paloma Picasso

Pope Benedict XVI

Quentin Tarantino

Sean Combs

Sean Penn

Stephen Hawking

Ted Turner

Willem Dafoe

Wynton Marsalis

Yoko Ono

*Inclusion on this list does not guarantee the celebrity will be present—only that said celebrity is alive and glamorous at the time of this announcement. Some featured names may receive a complimentary crypt as compensation for their appearance. For more information, please go to chuckpalahniuk.net.

Greyhound
Across America

WILLIAM T. VOLLMANN

I have been asked to tell you about some travel experience of mine, preferably an exotic one, and after mature reflection I've concluded: What could be more exotic than a Greyhound bus? It's true that the *taxi-brousses* of Madagascar take even longer, because they are privately owned; and each driver, happily smoking cigarettes in his mucky parking lot, will wait until the last smidgeon of human jelly has been packed into the can, top it off with another body or two, and then start off on four flat tires, five hours late. Greyhound can't top that, it has its own peculiar charms.

First of all, one can count on the presence of the pathetic and the angry. With luck, racial taunts will spice up the atmosphere. Drunken vomiting is rarer, but not so out of the question as to be undeserving of mention in this field guide. Now, of course, drunken vomiting can occur in other venues also. In Mexico, for instance, trains and buses are replete with loud talk, but it tends to be good-humored, drunken or not, and it is often inclusive: My neighbor, singing at the top of his voice, offers me a swig from a bottle of mescal. He wants to teach me the latest drug ballad; he sings me his favorite love song. That is Mexico. In America, my neighbor leans forward to obscenely threaten the single woman in the seat ahead. She dares not reply; I wonder how terrified she is. Who will do anything to help her? Nobody, for this is America, the Land of the Free.

The Greyhound is America: Every man for himself. In Belize, the man on the bus beside me tells me his life story, without hope or self-pity. On the Greyhound, my neighbor whines, threatens, or silently stinks. In any case, he neither shares himself with me nor asks me about myself.

I remember a time on a Greyhound in the California desert when another Greyhound on the road had broken down. Our driver stopped. He asked all of us to make room for these people as best we could. None of the stranded would be allowed to stand in our aisle, thanks to one of many exotic American laws, so most must remain behind; in Madagascar they'd all have crowded in somehow, assuming that the *taxi-brousse* stopped at all; come to think of it, it would have stopped. Anyhow, for the sake of the lucky dozen who could fit on our Greyhound, the driver requested that we take our luggage off all free seats, that mothers put their small children on their laps. And most of us were outraged. The driver came down the aisle, patiently repeating himself to those who hadn't budged, and mothers cursed him. He was white, and a black man who was taking up two seats called him a nasty racial name and threatened him. Nobody could give a damn about the people outside in the heat.

In Madagascar, when our *taxi-brousse* broke down, we all shared food, and nobody got angry.

Oh, I've made friends on the Greyhound once in awhile. I don't deny that. Sometimes I even hear good stories. Once in awhile, a Jehovah's Witness takes enough interest in me to try to save my soul. I'm not complaining; I'm really not. If I were, I'd be just like everybody else on the Greyhound, and I wouldn't want that, because I'm a snob. I'm such an elitist that I insist on drawing your attention to the man with redrimmed eyes who sits beside me muttering angry obscenities to himself all day and all night. I don't usually see his like on Serbian trains, Yemeni buses, Canadian ferryboats. I always see him on the Greyhound. That's why I consider him exotic.

Welcome to America. Onward, Christian soldiers.

Flower Hunting in the Congo

JT LeROY

We are beneath a canopy of trees so dense it does not seem possible that enough light penetrates to account for the thick undergrowth we are hacking our way through.

"Uh, how much farther?" I ask, smacking a dubious-looking blood-filled mosquito on my leg, trying to discern in its Rorschach splat on my palm any deadly diseases that might now be chomping their way into my bloodstream. I really try to sound blithely inquisitive, not at all whiny, not like I'd rather be back home in foggy San Francisco than in this jungle in the Congo. The business end of the machete carried by the man leading us swings a tad too close to my abdomen.

"You wanted adventure," William T. Vollmann reminds me genteelly.

"Oh, wait till you smell this flower! It will be worth it!" the lady merrily traipsing alongside Vollmann sings in her never-less-than enthusiastic voice.

Vollmann hacks apart a tangle in front of us and doesn't pause at the volley of gunfire, which I try to convince myself is really just branches beneath our combat boots. Like the fabled Native American listening to the ground to gauge the distance of the enemy, Vollmann reads the echoes of gunplay with a slightly cocked head: "Five miles off, southwest, opposite direction, warning shots. . . ." He notes the uncontrollable tremble of my hand as he holds a long bramble for me. "Not to us," he says of the gunfire. He shoots me what I am positive is meant as a reassuring grin, but being in the grips of fulfilling a passion, one can never be too sure. Assured confidence and maniacal poise can have mighty similar appearances.

I have done many extraordinary things out of passion, or maybe I am just confusing passion with obsession. I followed my mother around the country when it was clear she saw me only as useful in gratifying her addictions. I didn't care what danger I was in—from arrest, dealers, OD'ing. I felt the way a war reporter must: impervious—just here to be close to the subject, almost invisible, shrouded under the safety cloak of my invincible passion, perhaps addicted to the audacity passion leant me.

And here we are in the jungles of the Congo, a place of massive dangers, lured by passion. Perhaps to get away from the constant drain of my own, I have succumbed to the hypothetical passion of another.

When Mandy Aftel, famed Bay Area author and therapist of many a local writer, hears the warning cry of "Skunk!" she flares her nostrils and inhales deeply. She reacts to odors with that miasma that inspired some colonists to take flint to kindling for impromptu witch roasts.

"I love the intense variety and beauty of most smells!" she enthuses. "To me, it is spiritual. . . . If you didn't believe in God, the scent of boronia, ambergris, and jasmine would make you a believer. To smell these things is to be in the presence of the gloriousness of nature."

And thus, out of perhaps an extra chromosome, we have a super smeller, just as there are super tasters—those who taste way beyond mere mortal tongues. Mandy channeled this ability into an art form. She perfected the craft of natural perfumery so she could utilize her olfactory magnetism to hand construct fragrances that had never before been experienced, so she could revel in the rarefied scents.

Mandy ministered to me when my obsession with my mother could take my body no farther. I did not go to New Orleans to try one more time to save my mother the last time she called. I said no. Like I never had. Her passion for heroin could not be sated in just one mainline. I would never hear her voice again. What a surprise that an oil—sandalwood—could somehow soothe and bring me relief. I became intrigued by the exquisite fetishlike detail Mandy goes into to acquire a scent. It is the stuff of legend, and I would not put yak scrotum sweat gathered by albino eunuchs past her.

It is through her passion that I met a hero of mine. I'd read stories of William T. Vollmann in magazines I browsed through in adolescent homeless shelters. I sat in a plastic Day-Glo yellow chair and quickly became absorbed in an article on the war in Sarajevo, becoming numb when I read that two of the reporter's friends were killed in the car they were in. If Vollmann had been in a different seat, he would be among the dead.

I knew about the randomness of death, but to read about it so matter-of-factly, without self-pity or sentimentality or the self-castigation of the survivor, opened the door to possible strategies of fortitude. I followed Vollmann's adventures—rescuing a child in Thailand, joining the Mujahedin in Afghanistan—and read his eight-hundred-page masterpiece, *The Royal Family*, which unfolds in the underworld of San Francisco's Tenderloin. I read about how passionate Vollmann was in the search for reality, for truth in his storytelling—so passionate that he smoked crack to get it right. And as I started channeling my passion into books and articles, I met editors who had just published Vollmann, and I always felt that chill the captain of a small boat in thick mist must feel as the heavy wake jolts the vessel and he realizes just how close they were. But I could never bring myself past my awe to write him to express how, in reading about how he followed his passions all over the globe, to the most remote danger-laden corners, it gave me permission to stay put and purge myself of mine.

And it is a flower that brought us all together. A blossom, I am told, that unfurls the most heavenly scent humankind ever had a whiff of and leads to a hallucinatory reverie in which the truth of your being is revealed to you. A flower that is in severe danger of extinction.

Vollmann brought back one of these exotic flowers to Mandy after he'd been to the Congo to cover the political scene. Mandy tried to keep the flower alive after experiencing its mystery, but only a whisper of it remained in the desiccated leaves so sleek they shamed any silkworm's toil. She'd dreamed of this flower. She'd heard of its healing applications once applied, and the rumors of how pharmaceutical companies were looking to harvest the plant, to study and reproduce it in a patentable form.

When I heard Mandy and Vollmann were planning a trip to the Congo to rescue this plant, I had to go. I would go as a reporter, a role Vollmann would not be assuming this time. He would utilize his United Nations and press cards, but he was going as one who'd seen the Grail, who knew the path and what devils possibly lay in wait, and how to negotiate them. I would go as witness, as parasite, as adventure seeker—all I knew was the passion of rescuing this exotic plant became my own. And as Vollmann said in an interview, "If there isn't some barrier between you and the exotic, it's usually not exotic. What creates this barrier has to be either danger or difficulty."

And so, here we are, marching about in the Congo. Even as Vollmann hacks at undergrowth with a machete, he has an almost graceful, unassuming manner. He is unfailingly polite, he absorbs the customs of the other almost by osmosis. He instinctually knows how to employ the power of direct eye contact, letting the official's penetrating stare reflect off his glasses, his lack of eyebrows lending a mysterious aim to his own gaze, like a question mark without its defining arch, like a child. I wonder if he purposefully keeps his hands so impossibly soft, so that as he palms off the necessary bribes it is clear his are not the hands of a mercenary. It is as if his passion for extracting the exoticness of truth has trained him in the subtle art of blending and bending with the seamless strength of a ballet dancer. And it is Mandy's cry that catches my breath.

"The flower!" she shouts.

But all I see are the men in fatigues with large guns. And I am reminded of when I first laid eyes on their ilk at the airport in Brazzaville three days earlier:

As we descended onto the sticky tarmac, I pretended that the men with machine guns were just extras in a film, until it hit me—the odor of tension, the pungent sweat of those men swaying guns under their arms with the comfort children have with rag dolls. We had walked under their glare not with the tired excitement of tourists, but like guilty smugglers, eyes on our feet, trying not to attract attention. My body had felt foreign, all my unconscious mannerisms wrong.

I remember entering the streets of Brazzaville, and the sight of so many people without legs overwhelming me. As we walked, Vollmann explained the telltale signs of who'd lost their limbs to polio, who to a machete. A flock of children galloped past us in clothes that had been worn to the point of transparency. Their mouths were thrown open in excited shouts as they chased after a ball made out of knotted rags. I pictured all the vinyl and rubber balls my son has deflating in our closets and felt shame.

I remember telling myself, only hours before Mandy yelled "Flower!" that this was just a hike—like in the forest of Mendocino, California. But the distant whiplike crack of machine-gun fire mocked my delusion and, more than once, I pleaded to be taken home.

Now, as I sense the flower in my periphery, seeing such complex weapons gives me that strange, warm familiar feeling one experiences when catching a TV newscaster on the street, that feeling of vague recognition before it can be placed, that sense of, "Oh, I know you from somewhere, you must be a friend." But I remember Vollmann describing the RCD (Rally for Congolese Democracy) as Rwanda-backed puppets, and very, very dangerous. And I have imagined this moment: I would pull out my press card, I would take the bullet for them, I would be a hero. But the soldiers don't even look at me.

It is clear who they are focused on—who the real reporter is. Vollmann talks to them in calm, soothing French, even when their voices rise, even when a few rounds are fired off above us. I recognize the word *fleur* repeated.

Finally, after a long discussion, Vollmann turns to us and says, "We must prove what we are here for."

Mandy nods, and under the watchful eye of one of the soldiers, she opens the Birdseye Maple wooden box, the size of a record album, filled with three hundred vials lined in black velvet. As they watch, her skillful hands move swiftly as if in a street game of three-card monte. She holds up a vial and passes it to Vollmann. With his gaze averted, he bows slightly and passes the vial to the men. We watch as they cautiously pass it under their noses after first shouting what is clearly a warning to us against any trickery. And I'm not aware I'm holding my breath until their faces break into wide grins and the air moves back into me. Mandy is beaming, and I realize she'd been smiling since she opened her wooden box and began her alchemy—she knew there could be only one conclusion. She concocted many vials for the soldiers and their wives. Even so, we were allowed no farther. The flower we'd come for sat but five feet from where we stood. No amount of cajoling would move the soldiers. The flowers we sought were long gone, they said, even as one bloomed not beyond their shadow. They gave us papers that would assure our safe passage out of the forest. Vollmann tried one last time, nodded at their shouted responses, turned with a shrug, and led us away.

As we marched through the forest, disheartened by our failure, he started to double up with what I feared was perhaps a stray bullet. It turned out to be a long, relaxed, melodious laugh. He took a breath, and as he helped us climb over a swampy ravine, he told us what the soldiers had yelled: "They said we have too much passion and not enough brains."

We stood there for a moment, and as Mandy joined Vollmann in his release, it took me a few minutes to liberate the fantasy of shoving past the soldiers and saving the plant. It took me even longer to realize what was so funny.

POSTSCRIPT

We have no idea if any of the events recounted here actually took place. JT LeRoy claims they did. When asked for verification, however, William T. Vollmann denied ever meeting LeRoy, let alone traveling to the Congo with him. Confronted with this, JT responded: "It ain't fiction. He is doin' plumb too much crack. Everyone knows I just LOVE to travel and be out and about in the world! Why wouldn't I go to the Congo, one of the most dangerous places in the world, with him, to find a fuckin' flower?!" We leave the final verdict to you.

Ghostwalk

VICTOR BOCKRIS

The sickness of our time requires
That these as well be blasted in their prime.

—JAMES MERRILL

Everybody keeps saying that everything's changed. I think it's true to say that everything's *changing*, but everything hasn't changed yet. For the first time, Manhattan herself is my subject. Is she also changing? I'm just going to follow my intuition and see where she takes me.

I get on a subway at the corner of Church and Chambers Streets to see how near to ground zero I can go. I get off at Wall Street, the heart of the Financial District near the bottom of the island. I've never been here before, but I've come to test my left-wing values against the heavy-metal damage that's been done to all of them. I'm determined to make contact with the ghosts who walked these streets some months ago and to discover who is walking around down here now.

It's very hard to live in the present. It puts too much pressure on people, and I think that when you have people torpedoed into the present, screaming and hollering, and then you screw up their heads with a bunch of wild, new celebrities they suddenly got to start kowtowing to now—firemen and construction workers—it just flips them out. And I don't think anyone has caught this. I think we're really in a very dangerous place now. I believe we need the kind of intelligence and moral authority of writers and poets to tell us what's going on. As the excellent Beat poet Gregory Corso, who died January 2001, wrote, "when the world is insane/a poet/has got to be sane."

One of the major difficulties in negotiating this new relationship to New York City is that the weather is so beautiful. October is usually the greatest month because people have returned from their vacations and they've gotten back into their strides. All the best art shows and films open, all the major books are published, the entertainment industry shifts into high gear. It's the beginning of a school year for everyone, with all the clatter that goes along with it.

The heart of Wall Street—from No. Sixty, where I emerged from the subway, to No. Twenty-three—lies on the floor of a valley. This creates an air pocket, giving the street itself an eerily quiet tone that's backed by the constant hum of the traffic at both ends. By New York standards it's a short street—running only ten blocks from the East River to Broadway, where it ends abruptly—and it is also a very narrow street. Thus the stately skyscrapers that line both sides of it make canyons through which splinters of jungle light create a series of changing reflections on each others' walls. With their enormous military flags flying off of them, these are our cathedrals. The pavements are swept constantly by black men in neat red jackets. It's just a totally magical neighborhood.

Across from Twenty-three Wall Street, a white-shirted, jack-booted policeman with a restless Alsatian on a leash straight out of Burroughs stands staring down at us from atop the steps of the most ornate Grecian building, the Federal Hall National Memorial. George Washington took the oath as the first president of the United States here in 1789. An impressive statue of him wearing big boots and a big cape gazes downward, with a hand extended toward the Stock Exchange. I wonder what he thinks through recent nights, especially when he climbs down from his plinth and walks weeping through the blue dawn.

Suddenly, without any fanfare, an armored Jeep pulls out from behind the barricades in front of the Stock Exchange, followed by three inexplicably empty black Town Cars and a long black limousine, its window wide open, containing the president, the mayor, and the governor. It is a curiously elusive motorcade that seems to mirror the dreamlike silence of the street. It doesn't have any of the grandeur of Johnson's, Kennedy's, or Reagan's motorcades. There are no outriders on motorcycles, no wailing sirens. There is something terribly deflating about the spectacle. I want to see an exercise of breathtaking charisma. It's what Bush lacks most. I remember having the same reaction watching him drive to his inauguration. There were three empty cars then too. Nobody knew which one he was really in. He disappears without a trace.

I'm walking single-file at a twenty-five-degree incline upward to a barricaded pavement packed with people. We're headed toward beautiful Trinity Church, at Broadway and Wall. The noise is getting louder now because we're coming closer to ground zero and a hubbub of activity. Trinity's towering, medieval spire dominates the end of the street. It's got a portcullis-shaped gate that looks like a dragon's mouth devouring money or the entrance to a magical mystery cave. It is a majestic building surrounded by an ancient graveyard. A single ghostlike statue stands aching to speak in the midst of it. This is where anyone in his or her right mind would go to find peace in this neighborhood. (A bird sitting on a tree in the graveyard flies away.)

Slaloming around Trinity and down Rector Street, I'm suddenly in a silent death march. We're walking downhill looking at rumpled pavement along the south side of the church. The nicest thing about the area is that it's hilly. I am constantly going up and down little hills and around little corners. Walking these ancient, narrow streets is pleasing. They're on a more human scale than most of the city.

In direct contrast this zone looks like an armed camp now. Soldiers are driving by in cool Jeeps or standing in small groups around corners, repeating, "Sir, sir, you gotta keep walking, keep walking." Dylan has already written the soundtrack to these memories. Now I'm seeing more and more soldiers. I guess we're getting closer. Yeah, this is as close as you can get. . . . I'm at Rector and Greenwich . . . oh my God!

This is the first time I've seen it. Oh, you can really see the devastation. It's extraordinary. I'm looking at approximately eight stories of solid building charred, with hollow window frames, and an enormous mass of rubble on top that seems to have poured into a central cavity, that looks like a giant upside-down mouth. It's so still. You can't escape from it. The shattered ruin at the very center of the face of the building looks simultaneously like a broken fragile toy and an incredibly strong and twisted monster. I can't rip my eyes away from it. Holy shit! If Andy Warhol were alive today he'd be all over this, painting it in a hundred different iterations, because death and disaster were his themes over and over again. There's a spectral black veil over the ruined building, it's like something out of *Lord of the Rings*, a terrible disaster brought about by the world's most evil spider. To have walked down Wall Street and then come to see this remarkable sight; the whole story is right here, in the juxtaposition of the two.

At Washington and Rector Streets is the Cathedral of Death. A six-story-tall, framed structure of the columns at the base of the building. They look like a series of giant forks, or an Oldenburg sculpture, with about five stories of rubble behind them. It is the most chilling, beautiful, and certainly religious symbol of the collapse of the building, which was a cathedral of business. That's something we should now know. Yeah, my throat is full, I've been on the verge of tears a number of times, and I wonder whether I'm being soft. But I think not, because I've been reading Céline's *Journey to the End of the Night*, in which he describes walking through this same neighborhood in 1932, and I think I'm doing what he was doing, embracing the human beings. "I waited more than an hour in the same place," he wrote, "and then toward noon, from the half-light, from the shuffling, discontinuous, dismal crowd, there erupted a sudden avalanche of absolutely and undeniably beautiful women. What a discovery! What an America! What ecstasy!"

It's hard to find those beautiful women today. Everybody down here looks gray, anxious. Nobody smiles, nobody laughs, nobody talks; they whisper. I close my eyes, and for a second I hear them, the same beauties, the lunchtime girls, who erupted out of the Trade Towers' doors toward noon, filling the pavement I'm standing on, knocking me over with their high heels, their stockings, their skirts, their pale-blue eyes. . . . Aaaaaaah!

We are all living and continuing our minute-by-minute tortured existence, twenty-four hours a day, within walking distance of the mass grave of some three thousand (beauties among them) incinerated into dust. Surrounding buildings are coated in particles that were once people. A garbage truck pulls out of the zone with bodies in it. It's too bizarre. I can hear the whining of the saws cutting up the steel girders wrapped around each other in a nightmare vision of the impossible. This is many things to many people, but the overriding emotion is a heavy gray sadness among these ragged shadows.

I walked into the crumpled zone with all my values intact, I'm leaving it, face-to-face with jumbled thoughts. What did I leave there? Does music sound the same? Voices scratched by the ruins. And again and again the relief in walking away from it—sunlight on powerful majestic buildings topped by shining gold statues—and again and again and again, the shock of the new.

I come out of my reverie at the corner of Broad and Wall Streets, and this is fabulous, absolutely fabulous, and again I'm stunned. I'm back! Ah, you see, it's the dip. You come down from Broadway at about a twenty-five-degree angle and it is when you get down here to the valley floor of Wall Street that the sound is different. A whisky priest talks quietly to two policemen, a beautiful Japanese woman talks on the phone, and I wonder which lucky man is going to take those beautiful clothes off her tonight. Yes, I keep thinking about sex because sex and death go hand in hand at times like these. And I've heard that at night a lot of teenage girls are coming down, like prostitutes following an army, to scavenge for amour among the firemen and construction workers. And why not?

Because what we are trying to find more than anything else in this is ourselves. We are trying to understand who we are now, and it would be a mistake to think that we are a population defined by images of the celebrated police precincts or the cheerful voice of the elegant, mustachioed fireman. I think not. I yearn for the names I used to know. Where is Muhammad Ali, who has dedicated his life to forging relationships between America and the Muslim nations? Or Susan Sontag, who is one of our most consistently courageous writers? She wrote an analysis of our initial reaction to the tragedy, which she knew would be dangerous to publish and had the balls to say it in *The New Yorker*. That's the kind of heroism that I hope we can still recognize. If we lose sight of that, we really do lose sight of what this country is about. This country is not about the celebration of firemen; it's about the celebration of freedom. The most important freedom of all is the freedom of speech. Don't shut your ears to the words of the wise. My God, what happened to the left? Where are *our* moral leaders? Where are *our* spokespeople? I don't know what to do, I don't know what to think, I'm just a private. I didn't even make it into the Shakespeare Squadron. I'm with the Marlowe Brigade. But I'm still here, you know, and I want to say something, and what I want to say is: Where are the stars of these streets? Where are the lords of these rings? What are heroes?

I'm passing Sixty Wall Street again, where I first emerged from the bowels of the earth. This is the center of my walk, really, and I am just telling you, I can feel it in the pit of my stomach, I feel that I am going through a baptism of sorts: What we are beginning to see, I think, is not the rubble of two of our greatest buildings, but rather a religious shrine. And a grave of about three thousand of the bravest.

Those people were heroes because getting up and going to work five days a week, day in and day out, week after week, year after year, in a competitive and mercurial business with no security, always trying to make ends meet, having a family, and—most of all—bringing up children is a heroic task in the United States. Because it's a frightening task, now more than ever.

People are constantly frightened now, but fear has always been the greatest control mechanism in this country and in any country. So let's drop this whole thing about the buildings. It has nothing to do with the buildings; it's the people in the buildings that we're looking at. That is the grave.

We're searching for our identity as a country and we're searching for our identity as individuals and I think that we have to see those things hand in hand and the best thing we can get out of this would be a better balance between those two things. Meanwhile, each of us has the opportunity to squeeze through this hole blown in time into the present, tense and alone, but swinging across the wounded galaxies.

See, living in the past we feel less threatened because we know what's going to happen. It's already happened. I try to get back there all the time. I'm still missing the stars. I wish film-noir star Richard Widmark would turn the corner with a gun in his hand. I wish Muhammad Ali would have called me when he was in town. It's time to hit the phones!

Now I'm exhilarated again. I am just crossing Water Street, going to the opposite sidewalk, and turning my back on the tragedy, slamming my feet into the pavement like rifle shots, heading toward the East River. It's a beautiful day, and the river is active. It reminds me of Hamburg Harbor. I want to get on a bright yellow boat and go out there right away to sail up and down the river. I want to see all the sailors on their great big clipper ships, sailing from the old land back to the new, forever young.

Seagulls scream out from under the East Side's FDR highway, which rises above us, sweeping traffic up and down the river. Driving up that highway curving around Manhattan, you begin to see the bridges at night like strings of pearls around Grace Kelly's neck. The past connects to the present. You think of Manhattan as a woman again. And that's when you begin to cry.

CONTRIBUTORS

Mike Albo is a columnist for *BlackBook*. His journalism has appeared in the *New York Times Magazine* and the *New York Observer*. He is the coauthor of *The Underminer*—a very "New York" satire about that "best friend who casually destroys your life."

Jonathan Ames is the author of the novels *I Pass Like Night*, *The Extra Man*, and *Wake Up, Sir!*, and the essay collections *What's Not to Love?*, *My Less Than Secret Life*, and *I Love You More Than You Know*. He is the editor of *Sexual Metamorphosis: An Anthology of Transsexual Memoirs*.

Matthew Barney is the creator behind the epic five-film Cremaster cycle, one of the greatest art achievements of the late-twentieth century. His work has been included in the 1993 and 1995 *Biennial* exhibitions at the Whitney Museum of American Art, New York, and *Aperto 1993* of the forty-eighth Venice *Biennale*, for which he was awarded the Europa 2000 Prize.

Victor Bockris has penned biographies of such twentieth-century pop icons as Lou Reed, Debbie Harry, and Andy Warhol, with whom he became acquainted in the 1970s. Bockris still resides in New York.

Ryan Boudinot's stories have appeared in *The Best American Nonrequired Reading 2003* and *The Best American Nonrequired Reading 2005*. His story collection, *The Littlest Hitler and Other Stories*, will be published in fall 2006.

Augusten Burroughs, author of the bestselling memoir *Running with Scissors*, resides alternately in Western Massachusetts and New York City. Both *Running* and his novel *Sellevision* are in production for film.

Christo and **Jeanne Claude** are perhaps best-known for wrapping objects and buildings, including the Reichstag in Berlin, and the Pont Neuf in Paris. More recently they attracted attention for the Gates, their 2005 project in Central Park.

Douglas Coupland is an artist and novelist, best-known for the 1991 novel *Generation X: Tales for an Accelerated Culture*, which coined the term "Generation X." His other novels include *Shampoo Planet, Microserfs, Hey Nostradamus!,* and *Eleanor Rigby.*

Meghan Daum is a columnist for the *Los Angeles Times* and the author of the novel *The Quality of Life Report* and the essay collection *My Misspent Youth*. Her journalism has appeared in *The New Yorker*, *Harper's*, *GQ*, and *Vogue*, among other publications.

Alain de Botton's work has been described as a "philosophy of everyday life." The author of *On Love*, *The Romantic Movement*, and *The Consolations of Philosophy*, among other books, in 2003 he was made a Chevalier de l'Ordre des Arts et Lettres, one of France's highest artistic honors. He lives in London.

Joan Didion was born in California and lives in New York City. She is the author of five novels and eight books of nonfiction, including *The Year of Magical Thinking*, winner of the 2005 National Book Award for Nonfiction.

Emma Forrest is a British novelist, columnist, and screenwriter based in New York. She is the author of *Namedropper*, *Thin Skin*, and *Cherries in the Snow*.

Damien Hirst is the British artist best-known for his Natural History series in which dead animals, either partially or fully dissected, are preserved in formaldehyde. He was awarded the Turner Prize in 1995, and now spends most of his time at a farm in Devon, England.

M. J. Hyland studied law at the University of Melbourne and now lives in London, where she is writing her third novel. Her previous novels include *How the Light Gets In* and *Carry Me Down*.

Naomi Klein is an award-winning journalist and author of the international bestseller *No Logo: Taking Aim at the Brand Bullies*. Translated into twenty-five languages, *No Logo* was short-listed by London's *Guardian* for the paper's First Book Award, and won the Canadian National Business Book Award and the French Prix Médiations in 2001.

Jeff Koons enjoys the distinction of being among the ten most expensive artists in the world. Celebrated for his extravagant, often kitsch, sculpture and paintings, which operate as both homage to, and satire of, consumer culture, he is a seminal figure in contemporary American art.

JT LeRoy, Generation Y's first true literary celebrity and the subject of intense speculation regarding his or her true identity, is the author of the books *Sarah* and *The Heart Is Deceitful Above All Things*, the latter of which was made into a feature film by Asia Argento. LeRoy resides in San Francisco.

Sam Lipsyte was born in New York City in 1968 and grew up in New Jersey. A former frontman for the noise rock band, Dungbeetle, he is the author of the short story collection *Venus Drive*, as well as two novels, *The Subject Steve*, and *Home Land*.

Bruno Maddox gained notice with his first book, *My Little Blue Dress*, a satirical jab at the popularity of the memoir genre. He lives in New York.

Glenn O'Brien has turned his hand to many things, including a legendary stint as music writer on Andy Warhol's *Interview*, hosting the cult cable show *Glenn O'Brien's TV Party* that ran from 1978 to 1982, and offering sartorial tips to the readers of *GQ* as "The Style Guy." He is also the author of *Soapbox: Essays, Diatribes, Homilies, and Screeds*, a collection of his essays.

Chuck Palahniuk is the author of eight books, including bestsellers *Fight Club*, *Choke*, *Survivor*, and *Haunted*, composed of twenty-three linked short stories.

DBC Pierre is the author of, most recently, *Ludmila's Broken English*, as well as the 2003 Man Booker Prize winner, *Vernon God Little*. He lives in Ireland.

Neal Pollack is the author of *The Neal Pollack Anthology of American Literature*, and *Never Mind the Pollacks: A Rock and Roll Novel*, containing more vomit scenes per page than any other novel in history. He is also the editor of a short story collection, *Chicago Noir*.

Bill Powers was one of the original editors of *BlackBook*, and continues to contribute to the magazine. He is the author of the novel *Tall Island*, and he has written for the *New York Times*, *Details*, *Vanity Fair*, and *Men's Health*.

Dana Vachon is a regular contributor to *BlackBook*, the *New York Times*, and Salon.com. His first novel, *Mergers & Acquistions: A Romance*, is inspired by unseemly behavior witnessed while working on Wall Street. He resides in New York.

William T. Vollmann, winner of the 2005 National Book Award for Fiction for *Europe Central*, is the author of eight novels, three collections of stories, a memoir, and *Rising Up and Rising Down*, which was a finalist for the 2003 National Book Critics Circle Award in Nonfiction. His 1996 story collection, *The Atlas*, won the PEN Center USA/West Award for Best Fiction.

Irvine Welsh came to fame with his debut novel, *Trainspotting*, a darkly comic portrait of a group of young heroin users in Edinburgh, subsequently adapted into a successful film. Subsequent books have included the short story collection *The Acid House*, and the novels *Marabou Stork Nightmares, Ecstasy: Three Tales of Chemical Romance, Filth, Glue*, and *Porno*, a sequel to *Trainspotting*.

Dirk Wittenborn is the author of *Eclipse, Zoe*, and *Fierce People*, which was recently turned into a movie starring Donald Sutherland and Diane Lane. He also produced and codirected the documentary *Born Rich*.

Toby Young is best-known for writing about Toby Young. He is the author of the bestselling memoir, *How to Lose Friends and Alienate People*, a tale of striving and failing in the shallow media pool of New York.

BLACKBOOK +
BLACKBOOK LISTS

progressive culture +
the essential nightlife guides

IF IT'S NOT IN, IT'S OUT.

BlackBook Lists now
include New York,
Los Angeles, Chicago,
San Francisco & Miami.
Order online at:
WWW.BLACKBOOKMAG.COM